Something Old
Something New

Something Old Something New

Surprising Wedding Traditions & Superstitions Every Bride Should Know

Chérie Sion

Copyright © 2017 Chérie Sion

All rights reserved.

Published in the United States by Kismet Print

No part of this book may be reproduced, stored in a retrieval system, distributed, or transmitted in any form or by any means, electronic or mechanical, including photocopying scanning, uploading, recording, or any information storage and retrieval system, or otherwise, without the author's and publisher's express prior written permission. If you would like permission to use material from this publication, please contact the publisher at cherie@kismetprint.com.

ISBN-13: 9780998866017

Library of Congress Control Number: 2017904985
LCCN Imprint Name: Kismet Print

Printed in the United States

Cover Design by Roberta Zee
Interior Design by Fifi Klein

Interior Illustrations by Dane Smith (pp. 2, 6, 8-9, 12, 15, 20, 22, 25, 34, 36-37, 44-45, 51-58, 60-62, 64, 66-67); all others are Shutterstock

First Edition 2021

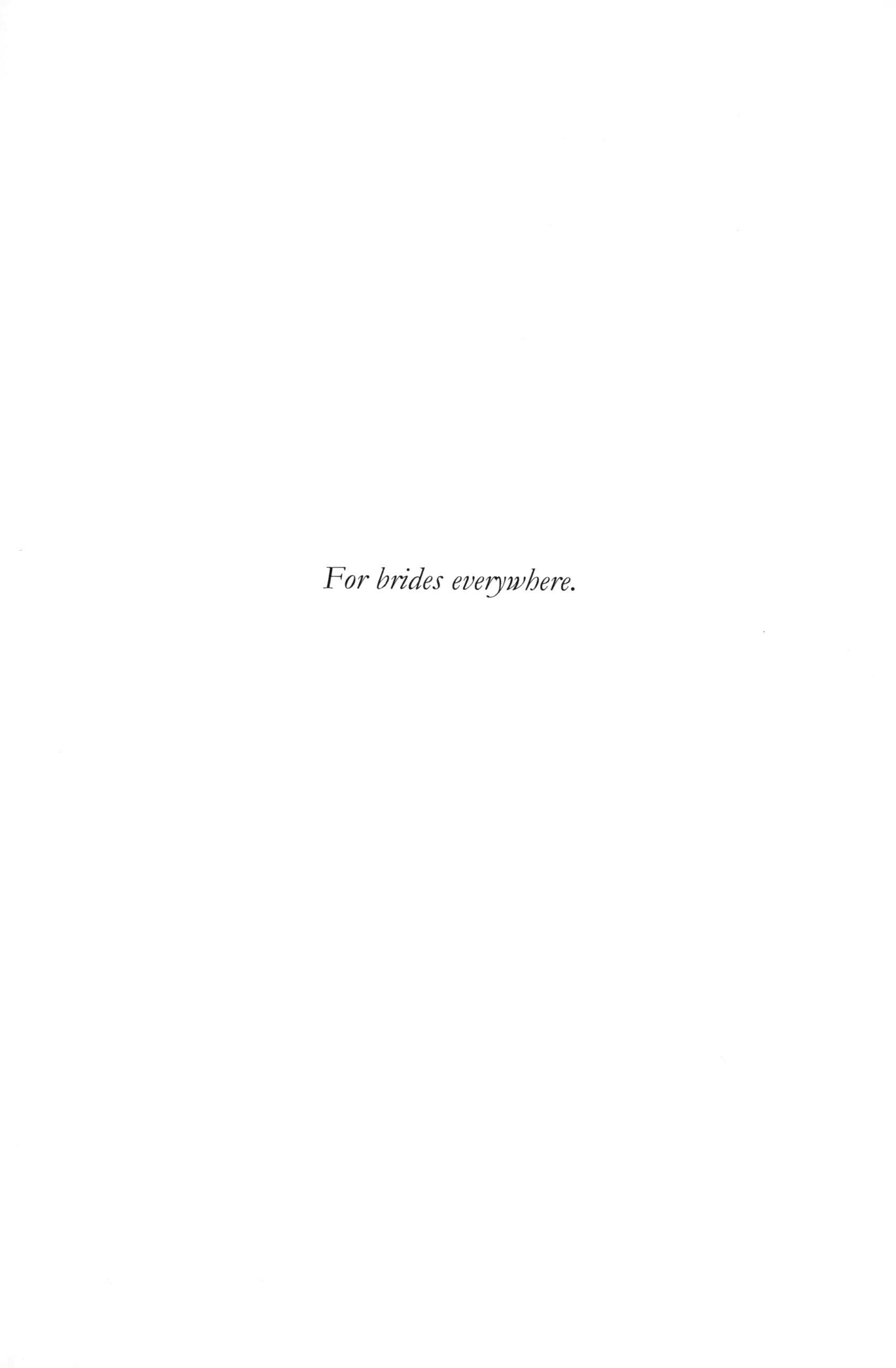

For brides everywhere.

Contents

PART III

APPENDIX

Preface

Dear Reader,

Something Old Something New began with my marriage on a rainy day in Istanbul. Neither my groom nor I understood a word of our Turkish language wedding, but we knew we were married when someone said in English, "Kiss the bride!"

Of course, marriage is a joyous occasion, but for a moment during our Istanbul ceremony, I wondered if wedding-day rain is a good or evil omen. The thought was over in a flash, but the question stayed with me.

Soon after my newly minted husband and I returned home to Los Angeles, I began researching the Western world's rite of marriage and the superstitions that surround it. This book is a representative collection of that research.

Our wedding customs reach back to ancient Egyptian, Greek, and Roman civilizations, deep-seated in their logic and forever hidden behind a curtain of folklore and fable.

Time has recast many long-standing wedding myths into cherished marital ceremonial customs. Shrouding a bride's face to safeguard her from evil spirits was the forerunner of our bridal veil. In the era of "bride by capture," bridesmaids guarded kidnapped brides from escape; today's bridesmaids protect brides from stress. Once, fathers bartered daughters into marriage in a process called "bride by purchase." Now it's traditional for fathers to link arms with willing daughters in their walk down the aisle to the altar.

My husband and I have a personal tradition. Like this book, our foreign language marriage inspired it. We reaffirm our marital vows every year, usually in a different city and faith.

The year after our Istanbul wedding, we had a "do-over" in Chicago in English. But the minister left out a few words I wanted to hear, so the following year in San Francisco, we had a third marriage. That one did it. I finally felt we had "tied the knot." The ceremony was so gratifying we resolved to renew our vows annually.

So far, we've said "I do" again twenty-nine times—from Vienna to Shanghai and New York to Buenos Aires. A priest, rabbi, iman, ship captain, and a Las Vegas "Elvis" are among those who have presided at our vow reaffirmations.

I'm writing a book (*Renew Your I Do*) that's based on our two-dozen-plus "marriages." There's a sneak preview in the back of this book. The excerpt is about our unintended Quaker wedding, a delightful experience that took place because I'd meant to arrange a Shaker ceremony.

Oh, yes! Some say you are only a bride on your wedding day. In my book, once a bride, always a bride!

All the best,

Chérie

P.S. If it rains on your wedding day, each raindrop is blessing your marriage with another day of happiness!

Comments and stories about your wedding vow renewals are invited! Contact me at cheriesion.com, cheriesionbooks@facebook, and cheriesion@Instagram.

Introduction

Most of us realize it's unlucky for a groom to see the bride on their big day before she walks down the aisle. But how many know why brides wear something old, something new?

Or for good karma, with which foot should brides take their first step into the church for the wedding ceremony? Or why are brides more likely to say "Yes, to the dress" if it's white?

Something Old Something New answers those questions and hundreds more about the Western world's marriage ritual while it guides brides through the thicket of wicked and good luck wedding superstitions.

The ancients made sense of their world through superstition and omens, attempting to control the uncontrollable and explain the unexplainable. In following time-honored wedding ceremony rites, today's brides unknowingly give tribute to those supernatural beliefs of long ago.

Is it irrational to honor wedding superstitions?

For her marriage to Prince Harry in 2018, Meghan Markle's wedding gown included pieces of the blue dress she wore when the couple met. Superstition tells us it's great luck for a bride to have a few of her hairs sewed into her wedding dress.

Grace Kelly, Hollywood's reigning queen of the time, had a penny under her right (instead of the traditional left) shoe insole for good luck when she married Monaco's Prince Rainier in 1956.

Have you ever been hesitant to walk under a ladder? Or felt a twinge of uneasiness if a black cat crosses your path? Or said, "Knock on wood?" All are relics of ancient superstitions.

It's not surprising that there are endless superstitions about such an epoch event as marriage. Some supernatural notions appear rooted in ancient civilizations' logic, but more of them are simply baffling. Regardless, many of those puzzling beliefs have become today's wedding customs.

The stories behind our most-honored wedding rituals are in this book's pages, proposing on bended knees to carrying the bride over the threshold. Readers will discover flowers' silent code of romance, if it's lucky or not for brides to wear gold earrings or pearls on their big day, and the direction newlyweds should face while sleeping on their wedding night to guarantee marital bliss and more.

Out front are the disturbing beginnings of marriage and how our modern-day ceremony grew from that start. Along the way, there's a peek into the *How Do I Love Thee* poem love story.

Backstories about bridal showers, long and short gowns, and the roles played by Queen Victoria, fabled fashion designer Coco Chanel, and Shirley Temple in shaping our wedding traditions are here. Sparkling asides about the Tiffany diamond solitaire engagement ring, the marriage ceremony's traditional "first kiss," and even the groom's tuxedo are part of the telling.

The wind-down is all about the wedding festivities: the reception, the newlywed's dance to the bouquet toss. Not to be forgotten are the wedding cake and the honeymoon.

PART I

TRADITIONS

"It takes an endless amount of history to make even a little tradition."

- Henry James

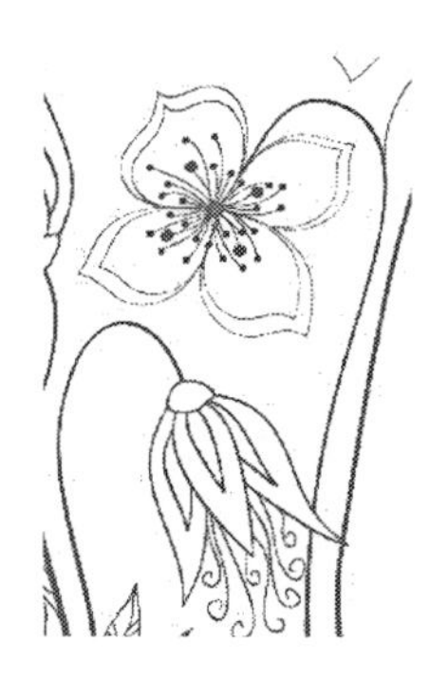

Traditions

Now we take for granted that marriage springs from romance and love, but that has not always been true. Initially, neither courtship nor love was part of our wedding ritual. Centuries ago, if women were in short supply, a would-be groom kidnapped his bride from a neighboring clan in a custom known as "marriage by capture."

Next came "marriage by purchase." The future husband agreed on a "bride price" (animals, land, or money) with the intended bride's father, and there was a wedding straight away!

For sure, there was nothing romantic about marriage by capture or purchase. So how did we get the wedding traditions we treasure so dearly? Most of them came from the practices and myths of the ancient Greeks, Romans, and Egyptians, restyled over many centuries into cherished bridal customs.

Virtually every bride incorporates one or more long-lived nuptial routines as part of her matrimonial ceremony, e.g., wearing something borrowed or blue, or carrying a good luck charm on her walk down the aisle. And, of course, she will join her groom in feeding each other a piece of their wedding cake.

In honoring wedding traditions, brides enrich the meaning of their marriage ceremony.

Behind each of our most lasting and often touching marital rites, there's a story. And they're all here.

CHAPTER 1

Popping the Question: The Engagement

Asking for the bride's hand

The modern-day marriage proposal is the equivalent of two rituals from long ago: *asking for the bride's hand* and *joining of hands*, both referring to the formal union of a man and woman.

"Asking for the bride's hand" refers to "handfasting," a custom that goes back as far as 800 B.C., the time of the Celtics, people who migrated from northern and central Europe to Britain and Ireland.

Handfasting involves tying the couple's hands together to symbolize the binding of two lives. The word *handfasting* comes from an Old English word meaning "fasten, bind, or tie," thus the phrases "bonds of matrimony" and "tying the knot!" Today, many brides and grooms include handfasting as a valued part of their wedding ceremony.

Joining of hands is associated with the privileged class of ancient Rome—the elites—who married only within their ranks and with the gods' consent. Authority over the bride passed from her family to the husband, who in effect became her master.

On bended knee

The "when and how" kneeling to propose marriage began is unknown, but the tradition is centuries old. The practice was common throughout the Middle Ages when chivalry and formal courtship still ruled.

Lovers of the past may have taken a page from legendary King Arthur's knights, who knelt on their left knee in front of their lady at tournaments to show their admiration and pledge to protect her.

Today, when a lover on bended knee proposes, the gentlemanly pose reinforces the proposal's social importance.

While kneeling to propose marriage is traditional, imagination in asking "Will you marry me?" does not lessen the commitment and devotion conveyed.

Widower Thomas Edison, inventor of the telegraph, the electric light bulb, the motion picture camera, and hundreds of other devices, popped the question to his second wife, Mina Miller, by tapping it in Morse code on her palm. She tapped back in his palm, "Yes."

Nowadays, originality in marriage proposals is commonplace. Romantics spell out "Will you marry me" in big letters in the sky, on signboards, and on scoreboards. Measured by such imagination, Edison's marriage proposal was humdrum.

In private or public, a proposal of marriage is a romantic moment that becomes a treasured memory.

Winston Churchill made proposals of marriage to three different women, all of whom refused. On his fourth try, Clementine Hozier agreed to become his wife. Churchill said his most brilliant achievement was persuading Clementine to marry him.

Leap year

Legend has it that women may propose to men on leap day, February 29 (also known as "bachelor's day"). Many advocate the elimination of the custom because they consider the idea anti-feminist.

Several stories surround the origins of the leap day tradition. One tale dates back to the fifth century when St. Brigid of Kildare complained to St. Patrick, the primary patron saint of Ireland, that men were taking too long to propose marriage.

In sympathy, St. Patrick named February 29 as the time women could propose. On that day, several years later, St. Brigid dropped to a knee and asked St. Patrick to marry her. He declined but gave the lady a kiss and a silk gown to help mend her broken heart.

Another version involves Queen Margaret of Scotland. Supposedly, Margaret passed a law allowing women to propose marriage throughout a leap year, but they had to wear a red petticoat while proposing! If a man turned down a lady, he risked a fine that could range from a kiss to the purchase of a silk dress or twelve pairs of gloves—one pair for each month to hide the spurned proposer's "ring-less" finger.

Britain's teenage Queen Victoria proposed marriage to Prince Albert five days after he arrived at Windsor Castle. As a reigning monarch, protocol required Victoria to be the one suggesting marriage.

Engagement announcements

In the first part of the twentieth century, engaged couples sent a specially designed notice to family and friends announcing their engagement. (Before the 1900s, only Christmas and New Year's cards were available for sending personal messages.) Typically, the designer announcements contained a printed message in verse similar to this:

Too good to keep our secret,
That's why we're telling you
The news of our engagement
And happiness so true.

Social grace called for recipients to answer an engagement announcement card with a written response. But companies soon offered ready-to-send cards acknowledging an engagement, replacing the need for a written reply. The professionally designed versions would contain a message in flowery verse, like this:

There's a certain happy sparkle
That just radiates from you,
And it makes a lot of other folks
Especially happy too.
May it mean the glad beginning
Of a life that's richly blessed
With all that means the most to you
And the one you love the best.

Engagement parties

Early on, betrothal parties were a prelude to and had the same reason as modern-day engagement parties: public recognition of a couple's commitment to marry and the joining of two families. But historically, betrothal conveyed a more meaningful meaning than engagement, i.e., a civil contract versus a promise to marry.

When engagement parties first began, the guests didn't know the event's purpose before arriving. At the appointed time during the gathering, the host would announce the upcoming wedding. Today, the secrecy is gone, and the agreement to marry is merely an excuse to celebrate—without the need of the "engagement party" label.

At one time in America, a law called "breach of promise" provided the right to sue someone for breaking an engagement. Most states have abolished these lawsuits. Still, the press reports that a Georgia woman won a fifty-thousand-dollar judgment in 2013 against her fiancée for breaking their agreement to marry.

CHAPTER 2

Engagement Blings: The Ring

About engagement rings

> *As she rescued a stunning fifteen-carat marquise-cut diamond ring from her martini glass—a gift from her third fiancé—film actress Lana Turner declared, "There's something awfully compelling about a large engagement ring!"*

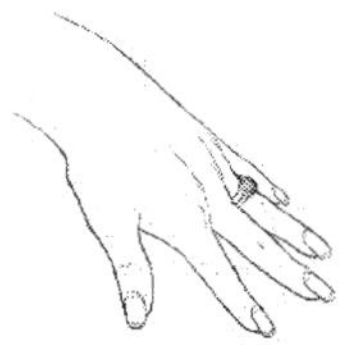

Accepting an engagement ring signifies two lovers' shared promise to marry and celebrates their new relationship.

Many generations ago, less wealthy grooms broke a coin in two, keeping one half and giving the other to their future bride. With oaths and prayers said over the coins, the couples understood "they would make what was broken, whole." Until they married, the woman wore half of the coin as a lucky charm around her neck to protect her from evil spirits.

In 860, Pope Nicholas I proclaimed that accepting an engagement ring represented an official declaration to marry. The ring had to have significant value to confirm the future husband was financially secure.

Three hundred years after Nicholas's engagement decree, Pope Innocent III required a waiting period between an engagement and the marriage. As a result, engagement rings gained status.

Before the 1800s, women wore engagement rings on their right hand. The groom moved the betrothal band to the bride's left hand during the marriage ceremony.

Etiquette asserted that if the man backed out of the engagement, the woman could keep the ring. But she had to return it if she broke the promise to marry.

> *Zza Zza Gabor, movie glamor queen of the 1950s, stated she never hated a man enough to give him his diamond back! Zza Zza married nine times.*

The diamond ring

In 1477, Roman Emperor Archduke Maximillian of Austria wanted to marry Mary of Burgundy but feared rejection. Advisors suggested the emperor offer Mary a diamond ring. He did, and she said, "Yes." Mary is thought to be the first woman to receive a diamond engagement ring!

The emperor's gift inspired the nobility and European aristocracy to give diamond engagement rings to their fiancées. Still, it took a few more centuries before diamond rings became the popular choice for engagements.

> *"Diamond" comes from the Greek word for "unconquerable," perhaps because the stone is the hardest gem, or as sex symbol and actress Mae West declared, "[A diamond] is the hardest to get."*

By the Middle Ages, diamonds had become the preferred engagement gemstone. The precious stone's hardness symbolized eternity.

The ancients believed diamonds protected wearers from disease and evil.

Fifteenth-century Italian jewelers were the first to cut a diamond, releasing the stone's brilliance. The lapidaries claimed diamonds' sparkle came from the gods' "flames of love."

In 1886, American luxury jeweler Tiffany & Co. designed the diamond solitaire engagement ring, destined to delight millions of women. The jewel sets atop six prongs, allowing light to shine through it from all angles, and making the gem even more stunning. By the 1930s, a diamond was the most popular engagement stone.

Franklin D. Roosevelt presented one of Tiffany's first sparkling solitaire engagement rings to Eleanor in 1905. FDR upped the sparkle by adding six diamonds to each side of the solitaire.

Over a century after its introduction by Tiffany & Co., the diamond solitaire engagement ring remains a classic and a romantic favorite. The De Beers Mining Co. slogan of 1947, "A diamond is forever," cemented the appeal of the gem as a "girl's best friend."

England's Prince Harry included some of his mother's (Princess Diana) diamonds in the 2017 engagement ring he designed for American actress Meghan Markle.

The regard ring

Thought to be lucky and with supernatural powers to bless the couple's relationship, "regard engagement rings" came into vogue during the Victorian era (1837-1901). The first letter of the precious stones in the rings spelled out a word. For example, "dear" would be indicated with a **d**iamond, **e**merald, **a**methyst, and **r**uby.

England's King Edward VII (Queen Victoria's son) gave his future wife a "regard" engagement ring with his nickname, "Bertie," spelled by the initial letter of each gem: beryl, emerald, ruby, turquoise, jacinth, and emerald. (The letters "j" and "i" were interchangeable.) Edward was keeping with the Victorian custom of saying it with jewelry!

The toi et moi ring

The "toi et moi" (French for "you and me") is one of the more romantic engagement rings with its pair of matching gemstones set side-by-side. One gem represents the bride and the other the groom, the symbolic joining of two lovers. Legend associates the ring with good fortune.

Toi et moi engagement rings are forever linked with two famous couples: Napoleon gave Josephine one (sapphire and diamond). John F. Kennedy presented a brilliant diamond and emerald toi et moi to Jacqueline Bouvier.

The birthstone engagement ring

For engagement rings, no gem is as popular as the diamond. Even so, a birthstone is an excellent alternative; it honors a personal milestone in a bride's life journey. And like the diamond, birthstones have a royal association. In 1840, Prince Albert gave England's Queen Victoria an engagement ring with an emerald, her May birthstone.

Birthstones date back to the first century. The ancients identified a gem for each month, believing that each precious stone named shared its special powers with individuals born in that month.

Besides showing love, adding a birthstone to an engagement ring shows imagination. Whether for an engagement or some later occasion, a birthstone ring is always an excellent choice because the jewel has a folklore connection with good luck.

Various cultures associate specific precious stones with the calendar months. The most common are:

Month	**Birthstone/Alternate**
January	Garnet
February	Amethyst
March	Bloodstone/Aquamarine
April	Diamond
May	Emerald
June	Pearl/Moonstone or Alexandrite
July	Ruby
August	Sardonyx/Peridot/Carnelian
September	Sapphire
October	Opal/Tourmaline
November	Topaz/Citrine
December	Turquoise/Lapis Lazuli/Zircon

The National Association of Jewelers adopted and approved the official birthstone list in Kansas City in 1912.

CHAPTER 3

In the Know: Spreading the News

Marriage announcements

Public notices of intent to marry go back nearly a thousand years when hired town criers shouted out who, where, and when the event was to occur. Effectively, all in earshot of the announcement were invited to attend the ceremony.

In 1215, Pope Innocent III proclaimed that all couples openly declare in church their intention to wed three Sundays in a row, giving the community a chance to protest. The words "speak now or forever hold your peace" constituted the last call for any objections to the upcoming marriage!

By the early 1700s, newspapers in Europe and the American colonies began publishing wedding announcements. These notices, in archived newspapers, are rich sources of information, especially since several American states didn't keep marriage records before the 1900s.

Wedding invitations

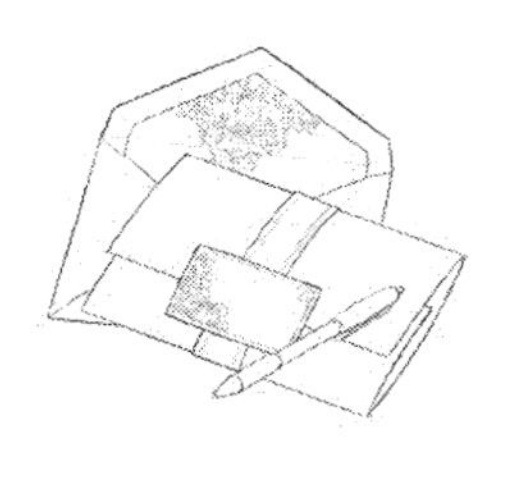

At first, people gave wedding invitations and announcements verbally. Movable-type printers made formal invitations trendy in the sixteenth century. Couriers on horseback hand-delivered the requests, each inside a second envelope as protection against dirt.

As late as 1789, there were only seventy-five post offices serving almost four million Americans.

Early American society followed the British wedding invitation model in format and spelling: "request the honour (sic) of your presence at half after seven o'clock."

Before printing presses, hosts placed a piece of tissue atop each handwritten invitation to keep the ink from smudging. (Formal etiquette still calls for the same procedure.)

Including an R.S.V.P. (short for the French request, répondez s'il vous plaît, "please respond") card made it easy to reply promptly to an invitation.

Each invitation came with a card with a pew number to hand to the ushers. The requirement of a "ticket" to enter kept crashers away. Each invite would also include or omit a reception card if space or other considerations limited the reception count. (An even number of guests guaranteed good luck!)

Marriage cards

In the 1900s, it was customary to recognize and congratulate newlyweds by sending the couple a "marriage card." The cards ranged in price from five cents to a dollar for one professionally designed ($1 in 1900 is equivalent to $32.14 in 2021 in buying power).

Typically, a picture of a bride's bouquet graced the card's front with a happy sentiment inside, like this:

Congratulations to you both
The best of wishes, too,
May the coming years hold everything
That means the most to you.

Bridal registries

Before registries, people purchased wedding gifts according to their best guess. The engaged couple had no input regarding the choice of presents, and it was impolite to make suggestions.

Years ago, if the bride received duplicates or gifts she disliked, etiquette required her to ask permission of the giver to exchange them.

Chicago's Marshall Fields (now Macy's State Street) became the first to offer a bridal gift registry. The "Windy City's" famed department store started the log in 1924 so family and friends would know the engaged couple's choice for dishware, silver, and crystal patterns. (Presumably, the registry cut down store returns.)

Using registries is so routine nowadays that even members of royalty list on them. After their engagement in 2017, England's Prince Harry and Meghan Markle reportedly listed with the Soho House and Wayfair websites. (Harry and Meghan also suggested donations to several charities.)

Lady Diana and Prince Charles registered at London's General Trading Company. Their list included garden furniture, ceramic candlesticks, and a pair of breakfast bed trays.

CHAPTER 4

The Prelims: Pre-Wedding Celebrations

Bridal showers

It's a given that a bridal shower follows the public announcement of the engagement. But how did this tradition start? The answer may lie in one of two legends.

A familiar folktale would have us believe the first bridal shower took place in a Dutch village in the 1700s. Disapproving the marriage, the bride's father refused to provide a dowry for his daughter, prompting sympathetic villager women to give small items to the engaged couple to help set up their home.

Equally appealing is the story that engagement parties started in England during the Victorian years when friends hid presents in a parasol and opened it over the head of the bride-to-be, showering her with the gifts—thus the term "bridal shower."

Regardless of the Dutch or umbrella tale's truth, bridal parties have become a valued and sentimental part of brides' wedding memories. Party on!

Legend says that it's terrible luck to use any of the shower gifts before the wedding. For good luck, the first present the bride opens at the bridal party should be the first she uses after her marriage.

Bachelor parties

Most identify a bachelor dinner with rowdy gatherings of males celebrating a friend's upcoming wedding.

A 1922 Scottish publication was the first to use the phrase "bachelor party" in print to describe the happy get-together. Now, these celebrations go by many names: In America, they're "stag parties," Australians call them "bucks parties," and French grooms know them as "enterrent vie de garcon" (burial of the life of a boy).

The word "stag" personifies strength and vitality, consistent with the fourteenth-century English definition of a bachelor as a knight, albeit a low-ranking one. "Bachelor," denoting an unmarried man, wasn't coined until the nineteenth century.

Sparta, the city-state of ancient Greece, may have been the home of the bachelor party. Spartan warriors would hold a banquet in honor of a fellow soldier the night before his marriage. Customarily, the parties would last an entire weekend!

Arguably, the Celtics held feasts that predated the Spartan dinners by over two thousand years. Ancient Druid men, the educated class among the Celtics, had evening gatherings before a marriage. They were purposefully boisterous events designed to frighten away evil spirits.

Bachelorette parties

"Bachelorette parties" likely began during the sexual revolution of the 1960s, though they were not commonplace until the 1980s. Taking a page from their fiancés' bachelor soirées, engaged women celebrate their upcoming marriage by sharing an evening of fun with friends.

In 1940, newspapers described a Christmas-time event hosted at the White House by Eleanor Roosevelt for cabinet wives and ladies of the press as a "hen party." Since then, the term has been used occasionally in America to describe an all-female gathering.

Wedding rehearsal

To make it clear-cut where everyone needs to stand, move, and know what to expect, clergy members customarily ask couples to do a practice run an evening or two before the marriage ceremony.

Superstition warns that it's terrible luck for the bride to rehearse walking down the aisle. Preferably, a "stand-in" performs the duty. And, for luck, the stand-in bride should carry a proxy bouquet made of ribbons from the bridal party presents.

Rehearsal lunch or dinner

Years ago, when guests traveled to attend a wedding, the host served a meal to the tired group. According to legend, the noise of joy and laughter at the supper on the eve of the ceremony chased away evil spirits.

However, a small, quiet formal rehearsal lunch or dinner is probably an American invention cooked up in the late 1800s. At any rate, the affair offers an opportunity—sometimes the first—for the bride and groom's families to join in a fun evening before the big day.

The night before the wedding

The bride and bridegroom spending the evening before their marriage separate from each other may seem like a superstition, but it's a tradition dating back hundreds of years. After the rehearsal meal, the couple kissed and went to different quarters, not seeing each other again until their big day. Their time apart emphasized the sacredness of the approaching nuptials.

Gifts for the wedding party

The marital couple's practice of giving presents to wedding party members was well-established among the Victorian-era upper class. Grooms gave gifts to the bridesmaids and groomsmen as a thank you and memento of the wedding. They might have given small fans, lockets, rings, or bracelets to bridesmaids.

At their wedding, Prince Albert presented each of Queen Victoria's twelve bridesmaids with a turquoise brooch of an eagle with ruby eyes and a diamond beak holding a pearl in each claw. The colors were symbols of love, passion, and eternity. People considered the eagle the highest-flying bird, and therefore closest to heaven.

When future-president John F. Kennedy married Jacqueline Bouvier, JFK gave each of his groomsmen and ushers a Brooks Brothers umbrella engraved with his initials and the wedding date, "9/12/53."

Bride and groom wedding gift exchange

Although it is a thoughtful pre-wedding touch, the groom and bride's exchange of gifts is neither obligatory nor necessarily reciprocal.

Authorities on etiquette regard the engagement ring as the groom's gift to his bride. Still, a couple may exchange token presents, highlighting the significance of their wedding ceremony.

Typically, wedding gift-giving occurs a few hours before the ceremony, at the rehearsal dinner, on the morning of the marriage, or just before the honeymoon. Years back, a bridal party member hand-delivered the gifts or a heartfelt letter between the bride and bridegroom before the nuptials.

Poet Elizabeth Barrett may have sent the poem we know as *How Do I Love Thee* to groom Robert Browning the day they married. The poem was published after Elizabeth's death.

For sure, though, Elizabeth received this letter from Robert on their wedding day:

> *You will only expect a few words. What will those be? When the heart is full it may run over: but the real fullness stays within…Words can never tell you…how perfectly dear you are to me—perfectly dear to my heart and soul. I look back, and in every one point, every word and gesture, every letter, every silence—you have been entirely perfect to me—I would not change one word, one look. My hope and aim are to preserve this love, not to fall from it—for which I trust to God, who procured it for me, and doubtless can preserve it. Enough now, my dearest own Ba! You have given me the highest, completest proof of love that ever one human being gave another. I am all gratitude—and all pride…that my life has been so crowned by you.*

CHAPTER 5

Dressed For A Wedding

Wedding dresses

Before the sixteenth century, brides just wore their best outfit, often a dark skirt or suit, for their wedding. Marriages were simple family events. Brides thought buying a dress to wear one time was highly impractical.

Wedding dresses reflected the style of the moment. For years, long modest dresses were in vogue. Department stores' arrival in the 1890s meant women had a choice of bridal gowns, including less expensive copies of the wedding dresses worn by the rich and famous.

During the "roaring twenties" (1920s), famed fashion designer Coco Chanel introduced the knee-length white wedding dress. Soon, long gowns were "out," and showing legs was "in." After World War II, the mood became more conservative, and fashions mirrored the times—floor-length wedding gowns were stylish again.

Changing from a wedding ceremony gown to a less confining reception dress is relatively new. More brides are choosing to make a second fashion statement when taking their first turn on the dance floor or posing for more photos.

Wearing white

Though England's Queen Victoria wasn't the first royal bride to wear one, she sparked the white wedding dress revolution. When she married Prince Albert, the teenage Victoria wore a white gown instead of silver, the classic royal color. After pictures appeared in newspapers and magazines worldwide, the queen's white dress and veil defined the color standard for bridal attire.

Godey's Lady's Book, a popular monthly magazine of the Victorian years, called white "the most fitting hue for a bride, an emblem of purity and innocence of girlhood and the unsullied heart she now yields to the chosen one."

> *Queen Victoria loved her wedding dress so much that she and Prince Albert reenacted their wedding day eleven years later when photography had improved.*

Wedding dress train

Folklore supplies the original purpose for bridal trains: In the days of "bride by capture," the extra fabric covered up the tracks of the fleeing couple.

The bride's train attracted attention when Charles Worth, a celebrity fashion designer of the time, created an eighteen-foot train for Queen Victoria's bridal dress. As a result, the length of the bride's train became a status symbol: the longer the train, the higher her rank in society.

Lady Diana's wedding gown included a twenty-five-foot-long satin train when she married Prince Charles at London's St. Paul's Cathedral in 1981.

Wedding veils

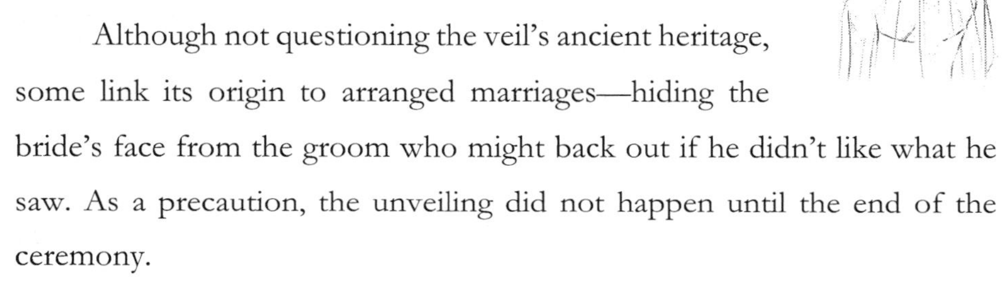

Over two thousand years ago, Greek and Roman brides wore long yellow or red wedding veils. The color stood for flames of fire, thought to ward off evil.

Although not questioning the veil's ancient heritage, some link its origin to arranged marriages—hiding the bride's face from the groom who might back out if he didn't like what he saw. As a precaution, the unveiling did not happen until the end of the ceremony.

Eleanor "Nelly" Parke Custis, George Washington's step-granddaughter, probably was the first to wear a lace wedding veil in America. Nelly wore it in honor of the first time her fiancé, Lawrence Lewis, saw her (through a lace curtain). Perhaps it was love at first sight! Remarkably, the couple married on February 22, 1799, Washington's last birthday before his death.

Handmade sheer veils were expensive to make, limiting their demand before manufactured lace. With the arrival of the industrial revolution's machines, delicate material face coverings became fashionable wedding attire for British brides of the early 1800s. The veils were considered synonymous with modesty and chastity.

Lady Diana wore a veil made of 150 yards of netting when she married England's Prince Charles. Known as a "cathedral veil," brides wear one only if they marry in a cathedral (a church presided over by a bishop).

The veil Lady Elizabeth Bowes-Lyon wore for her wedding to Prince Albert, Duke of York, in 1923 required 12,000 hours of work and 12 million stitches. (In 1927, the couple became Great Britain's King George VI and Queen Elizabeth.)

The tiara

Of course, any woman can wear a beautiful tiara (or diadem). Despite that truth, tradition stresses that only married women should wear one. A tiara signals the transition from a bride's single status to a married one. The headband, not to be confused with a crown, symbolizes the loss of innocence.

Tiaras go back to the ancient Egyptians and Greeks who decorated their heads with golden headpieces incorporating designs of wheat or branches of olives. Roman women adopted the tiara, wearing them as an emblem of rank. France's Napoleon and Josephine wore the headpieces as symbols of authority.

The popularity of tiaras has gone up and down, reflecting the mood of the time. By the late eighteenth century, tiaras were trendy. Renowned jewelers such as Cartier, Van Cleef & Arpels, Chaumet, and Tiffany put precious colored gemstones into gold and silver frameworks for European royalty, upper classes, and social climbers.

Tiaras didn't enjoy widespread popularity in America until the "roaring twenties," when they became fashion images of the times along with flapper dresses. For all of that, America's era of flappers and circlet headbands ended with the Great Depression (1929-1939).

While brides and women have worn tiaras and headdresses for centuries, those worn by royal brides attract the most attention. At her wedding to Prince Harry in 2018, Meghan Markle wore England's Queen Mary's 1932 platinum-and-diamond bandeau, which features a removable brooch (dating to 1893) in the center.

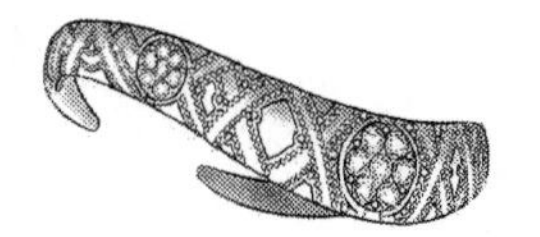

Something old, new, borrowed, blue

The saying that brides wear "something old, something new, something borrowed, and something blue, and a silver sixpence in her shoe" originated in the 1880s with the Victorians.

Something old signifies confidence that the wedding couple's dearest friendships will last. Brides frequently wear a piece of heirloom jewelry to symbolize something old.

Something new represents optimism toward a future of health, happiness, and success in love. Though the wedding dress or shoes often signify the "new," the most important new item is the ring!

Something borrowed is a show of family and friends' love for the bride. It might be a borrowed piece of jewelry, a veil, or a handkerchief. Legend says that if the jewelry is on loan, it should belong to a happily married friend or family member. To ensure good luck, the bride must return the borrowed item!

Something blue acknowledges the common belief that blue stands for faithfulness, love, purity, and fertility. Incorporating a bit of blue in the bride's wedding outfit may have originated in ancient Israel, where brides wore a blue ribbon in their hair as a sign of modesty.

A silver sixpence in her shoe refers to an English coin first minted in 1551. It is a good luck talisman for brides, assuring wealth, happiness, and long-lasting marriage. In keeping with superstition, the coin also protects brides from harm by a rejected suitor.

By custom, the bride places the coin in the heel of her left shoe. Supposedly, her foot's contact with money secures financial and emotional wealth in married life.

The garters

Garters go back to the Middle Ages. Both men and women of the time wore the narrow bands to hold up their stockings or socks.

In the seventeenth and eighteenth centuries, brides tied their garters just above the knee with long ribbons, making them easier to remove. The bands were like catnip to wedding guests, who treasured them as love mementos with magical powers. (People thought red or blue ribbons turned away evil spirits.)

The gloves

As early as the 1700s, brides wore gloves to signify marital fidelity. In fact, the hand coverings were fashionable bridal wear until the 1900s. Brides cut out their glove's ring finger to accommodate their wedding band. Omitting the "g," brides called gloves "a pair of loves."

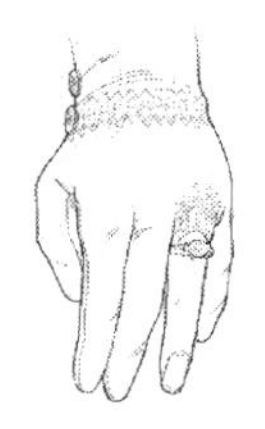

The handkerchief

On their wedding day, Victorian brides clutched a handkerchief embroidered with their maiden name or initials. (As if it were tempting fate, society disapproved of a bride's use of her married surname before the wedding.)

The hankies were a charming touch and came in handy for drying tears because friends encouraged brides to cry. Legend has it that a bride who weeps on her wedding day will never shed tears about her marriage.

Nineteenth-century newlyweds added ribbons to the bride's handkerchief, anticipating restyling it into a christening bonnet for their first baby.

The bouquet

Wedding bouquets have served as symbols of happiness for thousands of years. Early civilizations used herbs, e.g., garlic, sage, and dill, to make bouquets. The ancients believed garlic kept evil spirits away. Sage represented wisdom, and dill signified sexual desire.

When Queen Victoria used fresh flowers instead of herbs for her wedding bouquet, brides throughout the western world took note and began using flowers in their bouquets.

A bride's bouquet could convey a message by using the first letter of the flowers' names. For example, lilies, orange blossoms, verbena, and euonymus spell "love." The bouquet, composed of an odd number of flowers and wrapped with ribbons tied in "lover's knots," served as added luck for a lasting marriage.

History records that Victoria planted a bit of myrtle from her wedding bouquet in the castle gardens. Ever since, England's royal brides' bridal bouquets include a little myrtle from the queen's sprig.

Irish and Scottish brides often carry bells in their bouquets to frighten evil spirits.

The groom's tuxedo

Until the twentieth century, grooms, like their brides, wore their "Sunday best" to their wedding—usually a gray suit. Black was only for mourning.

By most accounts, the forerunner of the modern tuxedo was a tailless coat designed in 1886 for England's young prince, the Duke of Wales, better known as the Duke of Windsor (and briefly, as King Edward VIII).

One evening at the theater, the then nineteen-year-old prince admired the dinner coat worn by an actor on stage and had one tailored for himself. (Edward became Duke of Windsor when he abdicated the English throne to marry America's Wallis Simpson.)

As the tale goes, an American guest at several royal dinners admired Edward's jacket so much he had the tailor make him a copy.

With a satin stripe stitched to the pants' outer seam, the American wore his dinner jacket and pants to private events in Tuxedo Park, a onetime exclusive residential community (from which the tux takes its name) near New York City. With its lighter and less restrictive jacket, the classic design soon became fashionable formal evening wear for wealthier men on the United States' east coast.

The tux goes Hollywood

During the great depression of the 1930s, Hollywood's motion pictures offered an escape from the time's downcast mood, depicting glamorous lifestyles personified by filmdom's famous dancing duo of Ginger Rogers in a long gown and Fred Astaire in a tux.

Noting the Rogers-Astaire movies, Philadelphia tailors began mass-marketing the tuxedo. No longer limited to the upper class and movie stars, men from all walks of life could buy or rent a ready-to-wear tux.

The Duke of Windsor wore a midnight blue tuxedo that looked darker than black in photographs. Advertised as "blacker than black," the tuxedo color was identified with the former king.

The groom's boutonniere

Customarily, the groom wears a bud or single flower taken from the bride's bouquet on his tux or suit's left lapel and just above the heart as a symbol of love for his bride. Like proposing on one knee, the groom's boutonniere (flower) goes back to the days of knighthood and chivalry when a knight wore his lady's colors as a declaration of love.

CHAPTER 6

Cast of Characters: The Wedding Party

Flower girls

Centuries ago, young girls played a role in marriage ceremonies very much like modern-day flower girls. The girls, dressed in white to represent purity, walked ahead of the bride on her way to the altar, sprinkling garlic to repel evil spirits and scattering wheat, herbs, and grains in an appeal to the fertility gods to bless the nuptial couple with children.

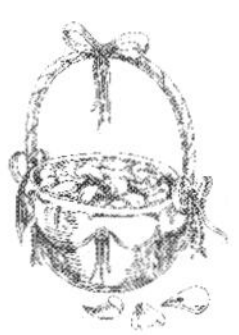

Nowadays, the flower girls' scented rose petals strewn in the bride's path are intended to assure a beautiful future for the bridal pair. The color of each leaf holds a special meaning:

Blue:	Hope
Green:	Youth
Orange:	Vitality/enthusiasm
Pink:	Sweetness
Red:	Love
White:	Purity and innocence
Lavender:	Charm
Yellow:	Friendship
Cream:	Appreciation
Peach:	Gratitude
Salmon:	Desire

Ring bearer

Victorian era pageboys bearing the bride's train, prayer book, and ring established the standard for current-day ring bearers.

> *Small children in a marriage ceremony procession represent innocence and a fresh start.*

Maid and matron of honor

Both "maid" and "matron of honor" titles carry with them essentially the same primary duties: Take the lead in planning the bride's shower and bachelorette parties, and assist the bride in planning the wedding and selecting the wedding gown and bridesmaid dresses.

Historically, a matron of honor was both a symbol of fidelity and a role model for brides. Only once-married women (with their husbands living) could be a matron of honor.

These principal bridesmaids, in effect, were the original wedding planners. They oversaw all aspects of the marriage ceremony—from the bride's choice of dress and managing the bridesmaids to flower girls and ring bearers.

Matrons of honor also served as guardians of the bride's bouquet, gloves, and "dow purse." (The dow purse was an agreed-upon trivial sum of cash—the first installment of "pin money" the groom gave his wife at the time of their marriage.)

Years ago, the matron of honor joined the bride and groom's right hands just before the couple recited their wedding vows.

Bridesmaids

During the days of "bride by capture," the groom chose the bridesmaids from his clan to assure their loyalty. To guard against a rescue attempt, the attendants escorted the bride on her way to the marriage ceremony. They disguised themselves by wearing the same color as the bride and carrying smaller versions of the bridal bouquet to confuse evil spirits.

By the 1500s, fighting off rescuers was no longer part of the bridesmaids' job description. Instead, their duties included making favors (silk knots with ribbons) and pinning them on guests' sleeves, helping the bride dress for the wedding, and removing pins from her gown after the ceremony.

Guests prized the pins as good luck charms, but any not removed from the bride's dress meant horrible luck for the newlyweds and errant bridesmaids.

Pins were lucky because all items made with iron would keep evil spirits away: "See a pin, pick it up; all day long, you'll have good luck."

Single women of that time welcomed an opportunity to be a bridesmaid because the role was high visibility, thought to improve their chances of meeting a potential husband. However, if she tripped going down the aisle or served as a bridesmaid three times, she was jinxed—hence, the saying, "three times a bridesmaid, never a bride." She could only reverse the curse if she were a bridesmaid four more times!

Best man

When marriage by capture was prevalent, grooms would choose their clan's most brutal warrior for "best man" to join in kidnapping a bride from another tribe. After securing the future bride, the best man safeguarded her from harm or escape.

At the wedding ceremony, the best man stood ready to help the groom protect the bride from a rescue before the couple's exchange of vows. Grooms stored weapons beneath church altars for quick access in case of an attack by the bride's family.

Groomsmen

Historians sometimes refer to groomsmen of ancient times as "bride knights." The knights joined the best man in safeguarding the bride from harm or rescue.

Like the bridesmaids, who wore almost identical clothing as the bride, groomsmen dressed to match the groom's outfit to confuse and guard against evil spirits.

The bride's father ("giving away the bride")

Nowadays, we view the father escorting his daughter down the aisle through a lens of pride, love, and sentimentality.

Regardless, the tradition is a relic from the days of *marriage by purchase* when fathers sold daughters to men who desired a wife. Then, a father walking with his daughter might have been to deliver her to the purchaser-husband in waiting.

A trace of marriage by purchase still exists in traditional marital vows when the presiding officiant asks, "Who *gives* this woman to be married to this man?" A modern-day version honors tradition but respects the equality of bride and groom with the question, "Who *presents* this woman to be married to this man?"

W | 33

CHAPTER 7

Put Another Ring On It: Wedding Bands

The ring pillow

Some speculate the Western world's wedding ring pillow is fashioned after the "crown's cushion" used in Great Britain's royal coronations. (After all, the bride and bridegroom are "royalty" for their big day.)

The British may have borrowed the idea of ring pillows from the Egyptians, who displayed precious gems on luxurious pillows to enhance the jewels' eye appeal and discourage people from touching the stones.

In King Arthur's time, the groom placed the wedding ring on his sword's tip for presentation to his bride. The blade was a symbol of loyalty, and when used to deliver a wedding ring, it represented fidelity and the sacred contract between husband and wife.

Wedding bands

As far back as ancient times, wedding bands have been a part of the human experience, a hallmark of love and commitment between two people. To the ancient Egyptians, the circular shape of a ring stood for eternity or the never-ending circle of life. The band's open space suggested a doorway to the unknown future.

Egyptians gave their brides rings made with bone, leather, hemp, and ivory. The Romans continued the Egyptian custom of giving wedding bands but upgraded the ring materials, using various metals, including iron, copper, and steel.

Roman brides wore a gold ring in public but slipped on an iron band at home for doing chores. The gold ring showed the groom's trust. The indestructibility of the iron band represented the permanence of the marriage.

In the late Middle Ages, alchemists referred to gold as the metal of the sun. Silver was the metal of the moon. They cherished platinum as heaven's metal because its color was thought to be a blend of the sun's gold and the moon's silver.

The ring's raw value with no decoration determined its worth, which equated to the groom's wealth and his depth of devotion to the bride. Gold, the purest of metals, conveyed the purity of love. (Like gold, love would never tarnish.) Silver, the most melodic and sweet-sounding metal, represented tenderness. Platinum projected strength and was the most valued because of its rarity.

Price made silver the metal of choice for most American brides until the 1800s. As gold and other gemstone sources expanded, their prices decreased, and gold wedding bands and precious stones became more popular.

Still, most English and American brides wore a plain gold band until the latter part of the twentieth century. Then three famous jewelers—Tiffany, Cartier, and Bulgari—began offering imaginative wedding ring choices and designs, from narrow to wide and flattened to fancy-edged, starting a shift toward expensive wedding bands.

The Puritans couldn't wear wedding rings, as jewelry signified vanity. Not to be denied, brides would snip off the top of a thimble to wear as a wedding band.

Blessing of the rings

As early as the eleventh century, priests blessed wedding rings with holy water and prayers. The blessing protected ring wearers from evil spirits and disease. By closing the ceremony with the word "amen," priests sealed the marriage.

"Warming the rings" is an Irish tradition similar to the "blessing of the rings." The bride and groom pass their wedding bands to the guests, who grace them with a prayer and return them to the bridal couple.

The ring finger

Ancient Romans and Egyptians believed the vein in the left hand's third finger was a "love vein" that ran directly to the heart, making the ring finger the most revered. Symbolically, a groom encircled his bride's heart with the wedding ring by placing it on her finger.

Double-ring ceremonies

Double-ring ceremonies are a relatively recent development. Initially, men considered wedding bands odd and unmanly.

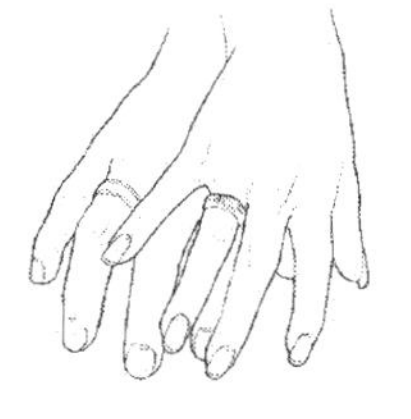

During World War II, Americans serving in the armed forces wanted a physical symbol of their marriage while serving overseas. That wish fueled a boom in dual-ring weddings in the Western world after the war.

Hollywood celebrity marriages helped make double-ring ceremonies popular in America. Tough-guy actor Humphrey Bogart (of the movie *Casablanca* fame) was one of the first high-profile men to wear a wedding band when he married actress Lauren Bacall in 1945. That same year, 17-year-old Shirley Temple married her first husband in a double-ring ceremony in Los Angeles.

Prince Harry wore a platinum band for his marriage to actress Meghan Markle. Harry and his father, Prince Charles, are among the few English royalty males to wear a wedding ring.

A worldwide television audience of over seven-hundred-million people in seventy-four countries watched Lady Diana and Prince Charles's wedding in 1981.

Ring inscriptions

The Romans were the first to engrave inscriptions on both the outside and inside of their rings. The wording often included the couple's names and wedding date or expressed a simple sentiment or love note.

In the 1800s, Victorians referred to ring inscriptions as a "motto" or "poesy." Customarily, they were romantic and flowery one-line messages, like these five:

In thee a flame, in me the same.

Thine eyes so bright are my chief delight.

As we begin, let's continue.

I will be yours, while breath endures.

God saw thee, most fit for me.

Noteworthy ring inscriptions

Englishwoman Elizabeth Maylan declared her eternal optimism with a ring inscription after her fourth marriage. She wore a wedding ring with the engraving "If I survive, I will have five."

Maylan's first marriage ended with her husband's death. The second time she married for money. Her third marriage was for the title (thenceforth known as Lady Cathcart). The fourth was for love, but it didn't last.

Alexander Hamilton, a Founding Father of the United States, gave a two-part interlocking puzzle ring—known as a *gimmal ring*—to his bride, Elizabeth Schuyler. Her name was inscribed in one loop of the ring and Hamilton's in the other. When put together, the two parts formed a single band.

King Edward VIII had one of the more famous inscriptions engraved on the engagement ring he gave to his fiancée, Wallis Simpson, a twice-divorced American. The message etched on the band, "WE are ours now 27X36," referred to the 27th day of October 1936, the date of Ms. Simpson's divorce from her second husband.

Marilyn Monroe and playwright Arthur Miller's matching wedding band inscriptions read "Now is forever" when the couple said their vows in 1956. Their marriage lasted five years.

CHAPTER 8

Retro Rituals: Standing on Ceremony

Ceremony locations

In the twelfth century, priests prohibited English couples from reciting their vows in church. The clergy required all marriages to occur "in the open" before noon and on a church porch. After the ceremony, the priest blessed the newlyweds inside the sanctuary with a Nuptial Mass. The church opposed evening weddings, denouncing them as an attempt to marry in secret.

As late as the 1700s, priests continued to promote their "beautiful marriage porches" for wedding ceremonies, even though they regularly conducted marriages inside the church. All weddings inside and outside the sanctuary were "regular marriages." Civil unions also were valid.

But society frowned on secret or elopement weddings and labeled them "irregular" marriages. Thousands of irregular marriages took place in the Fleet area of London, near the notorious Fleet Prison. Clergy members of questionable character were always around to conduct weddings for couples, who, most times, only had a brass curtain ring for the bride's finger.

If a Fleet wedding weren't the couple's cup of tea, a blacksmith at an anvil altar would do the honor for a small fee or a glass of whiskey. Besides, a "marrying parson" and rooms were always available at a nearby inn.

Scotland was also an option. The Scots didn't require parental permission, churches, or civil ceremonies for a recognized marriage. Couples simply declared themselves married in front of two witnesses. These marriages were available in Gretna Green, Scotland, just over the border from England. The equivalent of a quickie ceremony in Las Vegas, a Scottish wedding was an "irregular" union.

Early American weddings were private affairs, often held at the home of the bride's parents. Newlyweds announced their marriage before the church congregation the first Sunday following their nuptials.

At one time, couples exchanged their vows without a presiding officer in natural and spiritual surroundings, often on hilltops or in the woods where they felt closer to heaven.

Elopements

Now the word "elopement" suggests secret rendezvous and romantic escapes from disapproving parents. Yet, during the Middle Ages, it referred to a wife's act of leaving her husband to run off with a lover. Only generations later did the term come to stand for two lovers running away to wed.

One of the more famous elopements is silent comic movie star Charlie Chaplin's with teenage Oona O'Neill in 1943. Oona was the daughter of the renowned Broadway playwright Eugene O'Neill. The Chaplin-O'Neill marriage was a long and happy one, but Eugene O'Neill's anger never decreased. His fury was so intense he disowned Oona.

Poet Elizabeth Barrett's elopement with Robert Browning is also well known. Against her father's wishes, Elizabeth left home while her family was away and married Browning, a fellow poet, in a civil ceremony in London in 1846. A week after their wedding, the couple moved to Florence, Italy, where the two lived until Elizabeth's death.

The wedding processional

The music "Here Comes the Bride" brings to mind brides entering the church on their journey to the altar. It would surprise many to learn it is part of Richard Wagner's 1848 opera, *Lohengrin.*

Princess Victoria, daughter of England's Queen Victoria, was the first to have music during a wedding ceremony. The princess had both Wagner's "Here Comes the Bride" and "Wedding March," by Fritz Mendelssohn, performed when she married Prince Frederick William of Prussia in 1858. Before then, it was customary to have music only at wedding receptions.

Aisle runners

Yes, even aisle runners have a history leading to the altar! A white runner signifies a virtuous pathway, and a red one honors the bride while protecting her from any evil spirits lurking beneath her feet.

Wedding guest etiquette

Onlookers routinely rise when the bride enters the church center aisle. Standing is both a sign of respect and an opportunity for the guests to view the bride.

However, guests standing could be a throwback to the days when there were no pews to accommodate seating in the church, rather than polite etiquette.

Churches did not have benches until the fourteenth century. Once places to sit became available, wedding guests established a seating pattern that Christians still follow: Mirroring the bride and groom's spots at the altar, the bride's family sits on the left, and the groom's on the right. In Jewish weddings, the seating is reversed. Today most guests choose a seat rather than a side!

Positions at the altar

The bridal couple's places at the altar date to the time of "marriage by capture." With the bride standing to his left, the groom's right hand was free for battle if anyone tried to steal her.

Weddings vows

Vows are a couple's verbal or silent commitment made in front of witnesses. The mutual promises are a pledge designed to hold wedded couples together, regardless of future circumstances.

But vows were not a part of early marriages. During the Roman Empire, couples simply listed their property and signed a document recording the wedding as legal.

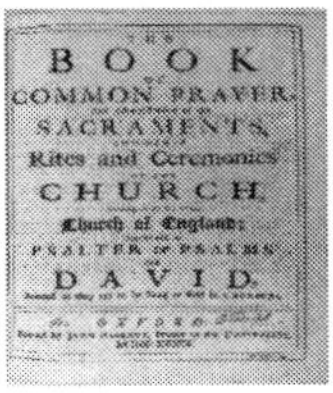

BOOK

COMMON PRAYER,

SACRAMENTS,

Rites and Ceremonies

CHURCH,

Church of England;

PSALTER or PSALMS

DAVID.

The 1549 Anglican Book of Common Prayer, published initially during the reign of England's Edward VI, is the basis for most of our present-day wedding vows. A single word in those vows—"obey"—caused debate among the English for the next several hundred years!

Churchmen revised The Book of Common Prayer several times until 1662, when separate vows for the bridegroom and bride were adopted. The bride's vows included "obey and serve him," which British queens and princesses dutifully promised for generations, but not without controversy from time to time.

The public and media criticized Queen Victoria when she promised to "obey" her groom during her wedding. As England's ruler, Victoria's promise suggested her husband might improperly influence royal decisions.

Similarly, the public expressed concern when Queen Elizabeth softly pledged to "obey" when she married Prince Philip, Duke of Edinburgh, in 1947. (Although spoken quietly, millions of Brits overheard Elizabeth's words clearly on the radio broadcast.)

Lady Diana and Prince Charles broke with tradition in their wedding ceremony when they used the alternative version of The Book of Common Prayer. Diana was the first royal bride to omit the word "obey" in her vows. Prince Charles and Diana said the same pledge to each other:

> *Wilt thou have this man/woman to thy wedded husband/wife, to live together according to God's law in the holy estate of matrimony?*
> *Wilt thou love him/her, comfort him/her, honour and keep him/her,*
> *in sickness and in health, and forsaking all others,*
> *keep thee only unto him/her, so long as ye both shall live?*

Diana's omission of the word "obey" seemed to meet with the approval of the presiding official, the Archbishop of Canterbury, who joked, "It would be a bad thing to start your marriage with a downright lie!"

Following in Princess Diana's footsteps, Kate Middleton omitted the word "obey" when she married Prince William in 2011. Instead, both Kate and William promised to "love, comfort, and honour (sic) each other."

Lifting the veil

After being pronounced man and wife, lifting his bride's veil is the groom's first official act as a husband. In earlier times, though, the matron or maid of honor would raise the veil before the newlyweds kissed, or the bride's father lifted it before presenting his daughter to the bridegroom.

The Bible's Old Testament tells how a father of two daughters veiled the older girl, tricking Joseph into marrying her instead of the younger daughter. As a result, Jewish grooms began lifting the bride's veil before the wedding to confirm they were marrying the right person.

The first kiss

There are at least two stories concerning the origin of the "first kiss." Most likely, the original wedding smooch took place in ancient Rome, when marriage was a contract, and a kiss was a pledge of loyalty and legal bond that sealed deals!

Customarily, wedding couples joined hands and lips at the end of the ceremony. The Romans believed a kiss commingled spirits, with each breathing a part of one's soul into the other.

France also gets credit for the "first kiss." As the last act of the ceremony, seventeenth-century priests gave a "holy kiss of peace" to the bridegroom, who passed the kiss to his bride. Also, the "holy kiss" may have been the start of the officiant's traditional words to the groom: "You may now kiss your bride."

The wedding recessional

Felix Mendelssohn's "Wedding March" is familiar to most of us as the music played on a church organ as a newly married couple leaves the wedding ceremony. As noted earlier, the music became popular as the recessional after Queen Victoria's daughter, Princess Victoria ("Vicky"), had it played at her marriage to Prince Frederick William of Prussia.

Wedding photography

The original cameras were too large and heavy to carry to wedding locations. To get their wedding pictures, brides and grooms would stop by a photographer's studio on their way to the ceremony.

When George Eastman invented the box camera he named "Kodak" in the late 1880s, people could take pictures with a "snap of a button." Before long, photo albums became common.

The Kodak gave couples (especially in rural areas) the power to capture weddings and other special moments on film. Many even took pictures of their wedding gifts.

With the upsurge in marriages after World War II, it became trendy to take pictures of the entire wedding. Still, the clergy remained reluctant to allow photos inside churches until the 1960s—and then, only at a distance.

Prince Albert's (later King George VI) marriage in 1923 to Lady Elizabeth Bowes-Lyon was the first royal wedding captured on film.

Wedding guest book

At one time, all the wedding guests signed the marriage form confirming they had witnessed the ceremony. The more signatures, the less chance anyone would question that the marriage was valid. This process, of course, led to today's wedding guest book.

Ancient Rome required ten citizens to sign a paper that they were present for the wedding ceremony to be a legal marriage.

CHAPTER 9

Now Presenting: Titles

Mrs. or Ms.?

When the officiant turns toward the wedding guests and introduces "Mr. and Mrs. John Doe," it's proof to the world the marriage is valid.

The order of words in the just-married couple's presentation comes from a superstition that "book-ending" the title *Mrs.* between *Mr.* and the husband's first and last names protects the wife from evil spirits.

The title *Mr.* is the abbreviation of *master*, which sometimes is used as an honorific for boys. *Mrs.* comes from *maitresse*, meaning "female teacher" or "governess."

Initially, *Mrs.* referred to a woman of higher social standing, an older woman, a businesswoman, or a female housekeeper in charge of the staff. *Mrs.* didn't signify a married woman until the late 1800s.

In 1901, *The Republican*, a newspaper in Springfield, Massachusetts, received an anonymous letter stating, "To call a maiden Mrs. is only a shade worse than to insult a matron with the title Miss."

Before the eighteenth century, "Miss" only referred to girls. By the middle of that century, it identified adult women, as well.

Introducing *Ms.* as the equivalent of *Mr.* took place in the early 1900s. The American business community encouraged the usage of *Ms.* to address a woman because it designated the female counterpart to *Mr.* and kept the woman's marital status private.

The U.S. Government Printing Office approved the use of *Ms.* in official documents in 1972. *The New York Times* announced on June 20, 1986: "Beginning today, the *New York Times* will use 'Ms.' as an honorific in its news and editorial columns."

In 1855, Lucy Stone, an American suffragist and abolitionist, refused to take her spouse's last name. Since then, the press sometimes uses "Lucy Stoners" when referring to married women who keep their surname.

"At home" cards

In the nineteenth century, newlyweds sent postcards to announce their new home address. Usually, the cards noted whether the bride was taking her husband's surname, hyphenating her surname with his, or keeping her maiden name.

The "At Home" cards also informed recipients of the days and times ("calling hours") friends and family could drop by to express their good wishes. Etiquette required the bride to offer the visitors refreshments. By the 1870s, the calling hours custom and the cards were no longer.

Chapter 10

The Reception

The receiving line

Superstition says a newlywed couple's touch is a blessing. A handshake in the receiving line provides guests with this lucky opportunity.

The "line" also allows the bride and groom a chance to meet new family members and friends, and to thank them for attending the event.

Proper etiquette dictates that it is appropriate for guests to offer their "best wishes" and "good wishes" to the bride, but it's rude and bad luck to "congratulate" her.

Only the groom gets "congratulations"—as recognition of his making such a good catch!

The reception

The wedding reception acts as the bride and groom's official welcoming as a married couple by family and friends.

At the outset, American wedding receptions, like the marriages, were small private affairs usually followed by dinner with close family members and friends. The industrial revolution (1760-1840) created a wealthier middle class, and receptions grew into elaborate events in church halls.

The end of World War II brought an improved economy and lavish wedding receptions at country clubs and hotels. Expensive venues, multicourse sit-down dinners with live music, and dancing defined social status.

Similar celebrations have taken place throughout time. In the 1500s, British and Scottish guests paid for admission to bridal feasts known as "penny weddings." The newlywed couple sold bride ale (bryd ealu), a kind of beer, to help cover the entertainment expense and supplement the bride's dowry. (The word "bridal" is a historically accepted combination of the two words, "bride ale.")

In the seventeenth century, a parade of minstrels, bassoon players, and drummers followed European newlyweds home from church. Food awaited them at their destination, where the guests enjoyed dancing, entertainment, and sporting games to celebrate the couple's marriage.

Catholics and Protestants fasted before the wedding ceremony in the 1800s. They celebrated afterward with a "wedding breakfast" at the bride's home. The term "wedding breakfast" actually referred to the first meal after the marriage, regardless of whether it was a light brunch or a complete lunch.

The head table

Originally, only the wedding couple, upper-class guests, and nobility had seats at the head table positioned on top of a platform. The arrangement gave guests an unobstructed view of the newlyweds. A container of salt, a status symbol of the time, served as the head table's centerpiece.

We follow the same protocol today: customarily, the wedding couple and honored guests sit at a head table in clear view of onlookers.

Salt was so valuable once that the ancients used it as money.

Wedding toasts

Why the word *toast*? In the seventeenth century, hosts placed scorched bread in each glass to cut the wine's bitterness. The newlywed couple would drink as quickly as possible because the one who reached the toast first would rule the marriage!

Legend has it that the ancient Greeks dealt with their enemies by poisoning them during a "friendly" meal. Understandably, wedding guests preferred the host to toast them by taking the first sip of wine to show it was safe to drink.

Toasts, in the opinion of Winston Churchill, "should be like a woman's dress, long enough to cover the subject, yet short enough to be inviting and enticing."

The couple's toast

The romantic toast the bridal couple makes to each other is one of the reception's highlights. Whether the newlyweds drink from a shared glass, tie their glasses together with ribbon or keep their arms interlocked while taking the first sip of wine or Champagne, the toast signifies intimacy, life, friendship, and the blending of two families.

Because of the herb rosemary's association with Aphrodite, the Greek goddess of beauty and love, servants rubbed the herb on the newlywed's glasses in England during the early 1700s before the couple's bridal toast.

Clinking glasses

Why do guests find it fun to clink glasses to get the married couple to kiss repeatedly? The merrymaking springs from centuries-old superstition. Creating bell-like noises with glasses kept the devil away, allowing the couple to embrace without harm by evil spirits.

The couple's first dance

A bridal couple's first dance, the sentimental highlight of the wedding celebration, dates to the ancient days of marriage by capture. The groom customarily paraded his kidnapped bride before clan friends, celebrating that he had a mate.

More happily, today's first dance is a nod to the couple's commitment to their shared life.

Vienna introduced the waltz as a newlywed couple's first dance in the early 1800s. The sight of men holding women with their hands around their female partners was so shocking that an English critic proclaimed only married women should take part in a waltz. Regardless, the dance caught on in polite English society. But American newlyweds didn't waltz onto the scene for their "first dance" until the mid-nineteenth century.

The father-daughter dance

Just the mention of the father-daughter dance brings to mind the charm, emotion, and show of paternal pride in sharing this long-established event. It is a public farewell from the father to the bride.

Today's image is in stark contrast to the dance's likely origin: during the years of bride-by-purchase, the father passed ownership of his daughter to the groom for something of value. Fortunately, not even its disturbing history can lessen the love and sentiment sensed by guests watching the father hold his daughter in his arms in their dance.

The bouquet toss

Credit goes to the French for launching the bouquet toss. In fourteenth-century France, guests thought any piece from the bride's dress, garter, or stockings brought good luck. To discourage wedding guests from tearing her wedding gown, the bride threw her bouquet to the crowd as a good luck souvenir.

Eventually, the ritual progressed to where brides tossed their bouquets only to single women. For the toss, brides turned their back to avoid favoritism because superstition asserts the bachelorette who catches the flowers will be the next to wed. If the bouquet falls to the floor uncaught, the bride will have awful luck in the marriage.

The garter toss

Throwing his bride's garter to bachelors is the groom's equivalent of the bride's bouquet toss; it is one of the oldest wedding traditions.

The garter toss likely was devised after male guests tried to steal the bride's garter as a good luck charm, often resulting in a free-for-all ruckus. In the interest of decorum, grooms started removing their bride's garter and throwing it to eligible bachelors. Whoever caught the elastic band would be next to marry.

Wedding presents

For all the money spent today on wedding gifts, the tradition had a modest start. Ancient Romans gave fruit to represent fertility.

Even as late as the eleventh century, friends loaned items to just-wedded couples with the unsaid understanding the newlyweds would return the articles after establishing their household.

In due course, wedding guests began gifting practical items to engaged couples. During the Elizabethan era (1558-1603), scissors were the most popular wedding present. They lost favor when anything that cut became a signal that the marriage would break up.

As wealth increased and social status became a concern, the value of presents swelled. Turkish rugs, a beautiful needlepoint, or a chest of excellent tea might be given as a statement of respect for the married duo's prominence in society.

Cash has always been an appreciated wedding gift. At one point, on the day of the marriage, it was commonplace for the maid or matron of honor and best man to stand on the front church porch asking guests for money on behalf of the marital couple. And the proceeds were the bride's sole property!

By the late 1800s, taking their cue from European royals, America's wealthy brides displayed their gifts to friends. Viewers saw everything: the trousseau (underwear, nightgowns, and garters), expensive and inexpensive items, and even duplicates.

Guests silently compared the presents, costly and inexpensive, and noting matching items—all presumably to the bride's embarrassment.

Vogue Magazine, an American monthly fashion and style publication, stunned famous designer Gloria Vanderbilt by printing an article about her wedding trousseau with a half column devoted to her lingerie.

When Prince Philip and Queen Elizabeth married in 1947, they received over three thousand gifts, which went on public display at St. James' Palace, attracting thousands of visitors.

Gratefully, by the end of the nineteenth century, the custom of exhibiting wedding gifts was boxed away and forgotten.

Wedding gift "thank you" etiquette

Etiquette experts say brides should send handwritten words of gratitude for wedding gifts within three months after the marriage. While American authorities approve the use of pre-printed notes, they emphasize brides should include a personal message of appreciation.

Here is an example of a "thank you" from a bygone era:

This message comes to bring our thanks,
Though words can't quite express,
How truly we appreciate
Your kindly thoughtfulness.

Wedding favors

Traditionally, the wedding couple gives their guests small mementos of the marriage ceremony. The gifts ("favors") are a way for the newlyweds to show their appreciation for the guests attending the nuptials.

Italian and Greek couples customarily give Jordan almonds coated with honey for favors. Newlyweds hand every guest five almonds in a box or cloth pouch fastened with a ribbon. Each almond represents a blessing: fertility, longevity, wealth, health, and happiness.

In France, sixteenth-century newlyweds presented their guests with a small crystal, tableware, or decorated container known as a "bonbonniere" (favor) containing a few sugar cubes. (Sugar was Europe's most expensive commodity and highly valued.)

In the eighteenth century, it was common to give wedding guests gloves as favors. Gloves were symbolic of friendship and reminders of the couple's marriage ceremony.

CHAPTER 11

The Wedding Cake

Before the tiers

As with so many traditions, the wedding cake's origin is a mix of superstition and luck.

Ancient Romans brought small baked goods of barley and wheat to marriage celebrations to break over the bride's head. Known as "crowning the bride," the custom predicted fertility and good fortune.

Scooping up whatever crumbs fell, guests ate them for good luck. These baked goods were the inspiration and precursor of today's wedding cake—with several modifications along the way.

During the Middle Ages, the English copied the Romans by piling sweet buns (coated with almond paste) high on a table in front of newlyweds. The bride and bridegroom would stand at opposite sides of the tall stack and try to kiss over the tower of buns without knocking it over. Superstition proclaimed success meant a lifetime of prosperity!

Puffery and pastry

In the fifteenth century, so goes the story, a French pastry chef traveled to England to attend a wedding and was shocked by the mass of tiny buns stacked in a high, haphazard heap in front of the bride and groom.

When the chef returned to his kitchen in Paris, he placed small cream-puffs (profiteroles) on-top-of-one-another in the shape of a Christmas tree and drizzled spun sugar over the "tree." The chef's creation, known as a "croquembouche," became a treasured traditional French wedding cake favorite.

During the 1700s, bridesmaids in England and France would eat a small piece of cake for luck after squeezing it through the bride's ring nine times (deemed a magical number). The tradition died out when superstitious brides decided it was bad luck to remove their wedding rings.

Of pies and cakes

The Victorians loved "bride pies," small pastries filled with minced meat, fruit, and nuts with a glass ring baked inside. If an unmarried woman found the ring, she would be the next to marry.

"Bride cakes" followed bride pies in popularity. The cakes, a single baked layer, had a blend of dried plums and other fruit inside, which supposedly enhanced the marital couple's prospects for children.

Customarily, seventeenth-century wedding celebrations served two cakes, a lighter pound cake honoring the bride, and a smaller liquor-soaked fruitcake celebrating the groom. Eventually, the groom's cake became obsolete, and the bride's cake moved to center stage as "the wedding cake."

Scotland's bakers introduced small charms with ribbons into their wedding cakes. The bride's attendants and single friends would pull them out. Each trinket held an amusing meaning for their future: a heart for true love, a horseshoe for good luck, a rocking chair for long life, or a wishing well for one's wishes coming true. A Victorian rhyme provides the meaning behind some charms:

The ring for marriage within a year;
The penny for wealth, my dear;
The thimble for an old maid or bachelor born;
The button for sweethearts all forlorn.

Royal icing

A foot-high sculpture of the mythical heroine Britannia (the symbol of Britain and its physical representation) and miniature likenesses of the married couple topped Queen Victoria and Prince Albert's wedding cake.

Only the wealthy of the time could afford elaborate wedding cakes, and only a master baker could make them. The finest of refined sugar went into the white icing, and, like Victoria's white wedding dress, the color was synonymous with purity and virginity.

Bakers called the perfected glaze "royal icing." (The word "icing" comes from a time when bakers brushed cakes with egg whites and sugar and placed the cake back in the oven to form a shiny finish resembling ice.)

What to do with wedding cake leftovers? Box them up and give them to single women. An old wives' tale predicts that if a single woman sleeps with a piece of wedding cake under her pillow, she will dream of her future husband.

Wedding cake tiers and legends

Two legends are everlasting about the tiered wedding cake's initial appearance on the scene.

An English romantic story dates to the late 1700s when William Rich, an apprentice baker, fell in love with his employer's daughter and asked for her hand in marriage. To impress her, he baked an extravagant wedding cake inspired by the shape of London's St. Bride's Church steeple. (Whether the young lady said "yes," is untold.)

A less warm-hearted account involves the debut of a three-tiered wedding cake at London's Great International Exhibition in 1851. The bottom cake layer was a real cake, but the two upper layers were fake.

Present-day three-tiered cakes take their design from the one served at the 1882 marriage of England's Prince Leopold to Princess Helen. The royal pair's cake was probably the first completely edible multi-tiered cake. The bakers made each of the cake's three layers individually.

Separated by a thick icing, each tier had a specific purpose: the bottom layer for the reception, the middle was a tribute to absent friends, and the top-level was for the christening of the wedding couple's firstborn.

By the 1940s, two- and three-layer wedding cakes became an iconic wedding symbol in England and America.

Cake toppers

Cake toppers, intended to represent the bridal twosome's togetherness, came into vogue in the 1900s. In 1927, Sears, Roebuck & Co. dedicated a whole page to them in its mail-order catalog, and by the 1950s, toppers were conventional wedding cake decorations and keepsakes.

These days there might be nothing on top of the cake, or flowers, or the marital couple's initials wrapped in a "heart."

The original cake toppers may have been the mini-statues of Queen Victoria and Prince Albert that crowned the couple's 1840 wedding cake.

The cake cutting

Cutting their wedding cake is the last traditional act newlyweds perform. It marks the official close of the day's festivities, after which guests who want to leave should feel free to do so. (Nowadays, the cake cutting often signals the start of partying into the morning hours.)

At the outset, the "first cut" was the bride's solo act, but all too often, the cake icing was so hard the task proved difficult. In a show of support and chivalry, the bridegroom would cover the bride's hand with his and slice the first piece together.

Cutting the cake together was routine by the 1930s. The practice represents the newlyweds' shared future and their ability to work as a team.

Sharing the first bite

The tradition of a bride and groom feeding each other the first taste of their wedding cake dates back to ancient Rome. Customarily, the newly minted husband fed his wife the first bite of the items prepared for "crowning the bride" as his pledge to care for her. In turn, the bride fed her husband a piece of the baked goods to show her promise to nourish him.

Saving the top tier

Folklore tells us a long marriage is guaranteed if the wedding cake's top layer lasts as long as a year.

In the early nineteenth century, some newlyweds saved the top tier (referred to as a "christening cake") and ate it to celebrate their firstborn's baptism.

In 1947, Queen Elizabeth selected a nine-foot-tall wedding cake weighing five hundred pounds for the reception following her marriage to Prince Philip. The couple kept one tier of the cake until Prince Charles' christening.

Keeping the top layer of the wedding cake for the couple's first anniversary became more common in the 1940s, when refrigerators with freezer sections became available to the general public.

CHAPTER 12

Wedding Rituals: The Before And After

The bridal trousseau

Trousseau is a French word meaning "collection of things" or "bundle," referring to the bag in which the bride carried possessions for her marriage, e.g., jewelry, lingerie, and honeymoon outfits.

In the mid-1800s, magazine and department store advertising urged women to assemble a trousseau—nightgowns, camisoles, corsets, and a special-occasion dress.

Harrods in London, Bloomingdale's, and Sears, Roebuck & Co. began selling pre-packaged trousseau sets, complete with nightgowns, undergarments, and travel outfits. As late as 1908, Sears still sold 12-piece trousseaus for $5.19.

Deluxe sets supplemented the standard trousseau package with a reception dress, stockings, walking garments, handkerchiefs, towels, and tablecloths. Stores even promoted "paper trousseaus" (stationery engraved with the couple's names.)

Hope chests

Hope chests go back to the days of the Egyptian pharaohs who stored valued items in jeweled boxes. These chests peaked in popularity during the Renaissance when European girls gathered essential goods for setting up a household in anticipation of their marriage.

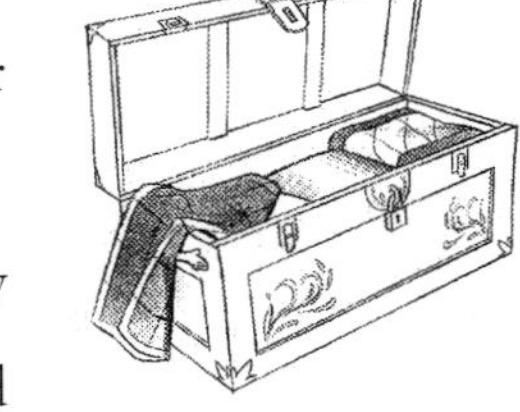

The name "hope chest" came into use during a time of limited opportunities for young women. For many, sadly, their greatest hope was for marriage.

A dowry chest, glory box, cedar chest, or merely the "bottom drawer" (as the English called it) served as a place where girls collected and stockpiled items such as linens and tablecloths, quilts, and cooking utensils.

Hope chests are mostly a part of a nostalgic past, nudged into the dustbin by bridal registries, inexpensive housewares, and other material objects.

Throwing rice

Showering newlyweds with bits of something is a thousand-year-old tradition. Early Romans and Egyptians tossed wheat over just-married couples to encourage fertility. Any grain, such as rice, corn, nuts, or oats, represented prosperity.

An exotic explanation for throwing rice comes from ancient Asia, where, according to legend, a lovely bride had chosen an unlucky day to marry.

For a moment, the bride was alone on her wedding day. A nearby golden pheasant, jealous of the bride's beauty, decided to destroy her. Just as the angry bird swooped in to kill the bride with its beak, wedding guests came to her rescue by throwing rice at the bird, chasing it away, and saving the beautiful bride's life.

The getaway car and bell magic

Honking horns, rattling tin cans, and shoes tied to the back of a just-married couple's car are all a wrinkle on age-old superstitions. Years ago, guests used horns and anything else that made noise to fend off evil spirits that might target a newlywed pair's open carriage.

People believed the full-bodied sound of church bells ringing after a matrimonial ceremony had sacred powers, shielding the just-wedded couple from harm. The chimes' reverberations predicted a happy marriage for the newlyweds.

Edgar Allan Poe's poem, *The Bells*, published in 1849, is a lyrical tribute to the magical power of tinkling bells:

Hear the mellow wedding bells
Golden bells!
What a world of happiness
Their harmony foretells!

As a gesture of good wishes, Victorian-era wedding guests routinely used footwear to bombard a just-married twosome's carriage as it departed the nuptial ceremony. If one or more *left*-footed shoes struck the coach, superstition said the couple would enjoy great fortune.

Once, shoe leather symbolized life and fertility, making it revered as a good luck charm. When the bride's father gave his daughter to the bridegroom in ancient Egypt, he also handed over her shoes. The act signaled the passing of his daughter's care to her husband.

Sixth-century Anglo-Saxon grooms received a slipper from the bride's father as a sign of transference. Shoes were a symbol of authority; a new husband would gently bop his bride on the head with one of her footwear, showing his role as head of the household.

Honeymoon

Origin of the word "honeymoon" goes back thousands of years when a couple celebrated their first month together at a secret location, drinking honey mead (a concoction made from fermented honey and water). Based on the moon phases, a couple's first month together was their "honey month," thus the honeymoon.

Attila the Hun drank so much mead wine at his wedding feast he died the same night.

During the early 1800s, well-off couples took honeymoons, also known as "bridal tours," sometimes spending a month in Europe or taking extended stays in the countryside.

Advances in transportation allowed middle-class newlyweds to plan shorter trips to nearby locations, often taking family and friends along.

Taking a "trip for two" honeymoon became more popular during the 1870s when advertising encouraged couples to skip the harassing bridal tour.

By the end of the century, it was run-of-the-mill for American newlyweds to change into "going-away" outfits, bid farewell to their reception guests, and leave for the honeymoon.

These days the end of the reception often marks the start of a planned or by-chance after-party bash that lasts until the dawn of the next day. If staying for the fun does not interfere with honeymoon plans, newlywed couples happily join in the celebration.

Carrying the bride over the threshold

First-century Romans believed evil forces could linger in a doorway. If a bride stumbled upon entering her new home, sinister spirits had taken control of the place.

To protect her from harm, the groom carried his wife over the threshold, avoiding the wrath of wicked spirits. And to assure good luck, he crossed the doorway with his right foot first.

Part II

Superstitions

"Superstition is foolish, childish, primitive, and irrational—but how much does it cost you to knock on wood?"

- Judith Viorst

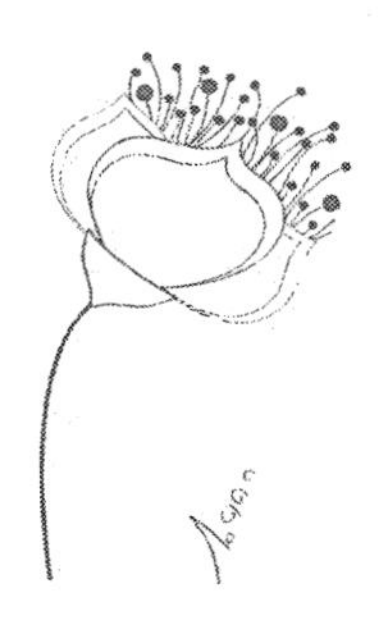

Superstitions

Superstitions about marriage are ageless, wrapped in fable and myth. Their origins lie in the clouds, rooted in legend and lore from long ago, and impossible to trace.

Even so, these mysterious superstitions gave rise to the wedding traditions that unite today's brides spiritually with endless generations of other brides...those before and those yet to come.

CHAPTER 13

Calendar Days

Engagement day luck

In the view of the superstitious, several times are exceptionally lucky for accepting a marriage proposal, notably Valentine's Day.

But if February 14 is too far off, Friday evenings are also fortuitous moments to say "yes!" And all Easter engagements foretell wealth in marriage.

Finally, accepting a proposal on a full moon day assures a happy wedded life.

For an extra touch of good luck, the one proposing should wear something blue, the luckiest color for lovers.

Engagement day crystal-gazing

Couples unknowingly flirt with wedding superstitions and omens from the hour the betrothal ring is accepted. An old wives' tale, preserved in the form of one-liner predictions, tells the couple's fate for every day except Sunday:

Monday:	The couple can look forward to an exciting life
Tuesday:	A peaceful and contented life
Wednesday:	A good-tempered relationship
Thursday:	The ability to achieve all you wish from life
Friday:	The couple will have hard work, but with rewards in time
Saturday:	Will give much pleasure

Oral history warns that buying the engagement and wedding bands on the same day foreshadows marital misfortune. More worrisome, if a bride loses her engagement ring, superstition says she won't marry the man who gave it to her.

Wedding month luck

Many regard June as uniquely fortunate for marriages, possibly because the month takes its name from Juno, the Roman goddess of love and marriage. Also, the longest day of the year is in June, making it symbolic of a lengthy and joyous married life.

Each month masks itself in superstition and myth, as shown in this poetic calendar from the past:

JANUARY
Married when the year is new, he'll be loving, kind and true.

FEBRUARY
When February birds do mate, you wed nor dread your fate.

MARCH
If you wed when March winds blow, joy and sorrow both you'll know.

APRIL
Marry in April when you can, joy for maiden and for man.

MAY
Marry in the month of May and you will surely rue the day.

JUNE
Marry when June roses grow, over land and sea you'll go.

JULY	AUGUST	SEPTEMBER
Those who in July do wed, must labor for their daily bread.	Whoever wed in August be, many a change is sure to see.	Marry in September's shrine, your living will be rich and fine.

OCTOBER	NOVEMBER	DECEMBER
If in October you do marry, love will come but riches tarry.	If you wed in bleak November, only joys will come, remember.	When December snows fall last, marry and true love will last.

Because May signals the rebirth of spring, many think the month is the chosen one for lovers. Even so, the fortune witches of long ago named May the least lucky time to wed, probably because the Romans called it "Maia," after the goddess of chastity, who caused conflict in marriages.

England's Queen Victoria, showing her trust in superstition, forbade her children from marrying in May.

Predictably, Lent—a period of abstinence—is unsuitable for weddings, as verified in verse: *Marry in Lent, and you'll live to repent.*

Wedding day luck

On the authority of an English legend, a couple's marital fortunes depend on the day of the week the bride and groom exchange marriage vows:

Monday is for wealth

Tuesday is for health

Wednesday is the best day of all

Thursday for losses

Friday for crosses

And Saturday, no luck at all

English Puritans honored Sunday as the time for worship. In the seventeenth century, following a strict interpretation of the Bible, they put a stop to Sunday weddings, believing it was sinful to be festive on the Sabbath. Ultimately, the six-day workweek made Sunday acceptable for marriage ceremonies.

Wedding day crystal-gazing

Luck is on your side if you marry on either New Year's Eve or the first day of January because both days "ring out the old and ring in the new." Marriage, like the new year, marks a fresh beginning.

The Scottish favor a New Year's Eve wedding. When January 2 arrives, the newlyweds celebrate their second year of married life.

Superstition confirms couples who wed on Valentine's Day will have a happy and prosperous marriage. The day takes its name from St. Valentine, the Roman priest put to death for defying Emperor Claudius II's ban on performing weddings for young couples.

By prohibiting marriages among the young, Claudius thought he could attract more men to his army. While imprisoned, St. Valentine prayed that a jailer's blind daughter regain her eyesight, which she did. Legend tells us Valentine left the girl a note signed, "Your Valentine."

Supernatural beliefs have many origins, including the stars and planets, on which mariner Andrew Waterman based his 1655 seafarer's calendar. Of interest (perhaps more to grooms) is the calendar's observation it's in the stars that brides are the "most fond and loving" on these dates:

January	2, 4, 11, 19, and 21
February	1, 3, 10, 19, and 21
March	3, 5, 13, 20, and 23
April	2, 4, 12, 20, and 22
May	2, 4, 12, 20, and 23
June	1, 3, 11, 19, and 21
July	1, 3, 12, 19, 21, and 31
August	2, 11, 18, 20, and 30
September	1, 9, 16, 18, and 28
October	1, 8, 10, 19, 23, and 29
November	5, 11, 13, 22, and 25
December	1, 8, 10, 19, 23, and 29

The groom's birthday is a lucky time to wed, except if it's on the thirteenth. But it's rotten luck to marry on the bride's birthday.

CHAPTER 14

Romancing the Stones

Gemstone symbolism

For thousands of years, soothsayers, philosophers, rulers, and the ruled have adorned themselves with precious gemstones. The jewels' never-ending appeal springs from their natural beauty and mortals' belief that the color of particular gems imparts unique energy to the wearer.

A favorite engagement jewel, the *diamond*, is an icon of eternal love. Folklore contends that the sparkling stone's "magical essence" possesses all other gemstones' powers while blocking negative energy from weakening those powers.

When a diamond is a gift of affection, the gem's magical essence is said to move from the giver to the recipient. But if the wearer purchases the jewel, the stone loses its powers.

A diamond represents the height of preciousness, although, despite popular belief, it is not the most expensive jewel.

Rubies, among the strongest of precious stones, are synonymous with love. Traded along the Far East's "Silk Road" as early as 200 B.C., the ruby is identified as the "King of Gemstones."

Ruby wearers supposedly receive vitality from the rock that keeps relationships passionate forever! Ancient Burmese soldiers inserted rubies into their flesh for protection from harm.

Dorothy of the "Wizard of Oz" movie (1939) fame wore ruby slippers for protection from evil forces.

Sapphires are second only to diamonds as the most popular engagement gemstone and a favorite among royalty.

There's a long-held belief the sapphire has a spiritual connection to heavenly harmony, apparently because the gem is remindful of the sky's color. The jewel's celestial blue suggests faith, enlightenment, and devotion to God.

The sapphire is thought to inspire love and was once royalty's preferred jewel. Sapphires possess positive powers: truth, honesty, fidelity, strength, durability, and good health.

Kings and queens of ancient Greece and Rome wore sapphires to shield them from harm. Long associated with romance and love, the gemstone's toughness represents strength in a relationship and marriage.

Princess Diana's sapphire engagement ring, surrounded by diamonds, is one of the world's most recognized jewelry pieces. Her son, Prince William, gave Diana's ring to Kate Middleton in 2010 on their engagement.

Emeralds are considered a hallmark of faithfulness, creativity, renewal, and protection. Kings and queens have worn emeralds throughout history. Ancient Romans made offerings of the stone to Venus, the goddess of love.

Venus' "sacred stone," the emerald, symbolizes devotion, revival, and security. Legend claims the jewel's green tint grants the wearer eloquence and wisdom.

Cleopatra's emerald mines in Northern Egypt allowed her to adorn herself and her palaces with the time's flashiest jewels.

Amethysts' transparent purple is associated with royalty. The stones, considered to convey openness and honesty, have a unique appeal: the gems are legendary for preventing intoxication.

Aquamarine is called the "treasure of mermaids." The stone communicates eternal youth, peace, and serenity. In the Middle Ages, soothsayers used aquamarines to foretell the future. The jewel's light bluish tint of green promotes insight, communication, and mental clarity.

Citrine is named after the French word "citron" (lemon in English). The gemstone's sunshiny yellow represents lightheartedness, prosperity, and self-esteem.

Garnet is the jewel of happiness. The gem encourages sincerity, unity, integrity, loyalty, friendship, and lasting affection. "Garnet" comes from the Latin word for the pomegranate seed, which the gemstone resembles. Supposedly, garnets reduce anger and encourage a logical mind.

The Chinese prize *jade* especially. Synonymous with good fortune, jade supposedly attracts love. Chinese wedding ceremonies feature jade, "a musical gem that concentrates the essence of love." Also, the gem provides wisdom in interpreting dreams.

Lapis Lazuli is the universal symbol of truth. The gemstone shows friendship, harmony, and fidelity. The Egyptians wore lapis during the reign of King Tut (the "boy king"), believing the stone's blue color represented the sky and the gold specks, the stars. Artists created the beautiful blues in Renaissance paintings with lapis lazuli.

Michelangelo used lapis powder for the blue color in the Sistine Chapel in the Apostolic Palace, the official residence of the Pope, in Vatican City.

Moonstone looks white at first glance, yet with a slight move, the gemstone displays subtle blue flashes. Fans believe moonstones bring good luck, especially for lovers. Supposedly, moonstones have intuitive powers, allowing the wearer to prophesy what lies ahead.

Morganite takes its name from American banker J.P. Morgan, who bailed out Wall Street in the financial panic of 1907. The stone's pale pink attracts energy, affection and delivers an enduring feeling of joy. Also, morganite nurtures trust in others and encourages fair treatment.

Opals are referred to as "Cupid's stone." The gem may be colorless or in one of a variety of colors. Opals convey desire, passion, fidelity, and luck when set as a birthstone in an engagement ring. The jewel symbolizes hope and purity. Beware, though—opals' ability to change colors suggests inconsistency.

Napoleon gave Josephine an opal named "The Burning of Troy" because the stone's array of colors captivated him.

Peridot, nicknamed the "evening emerald" because of its variations of green, attracts prosperity. The precious stone also ignites love, admiration and stands for purity and morality.

Pink Diamond's soft pastel color, expressing femininity, tenderness, and romance, makes it one of the rarest diamonds. Folklore says the jewel enhances creative expression. How the pink diamond got its rosy brilliance is a mystery and hints at a relationship full of pleasant surprises.

Admirers know the *Pink Sapphire* as the "intelligence stone" because it gives wisdom to the wearer. Its pinkness symbolizes intense affection, trust, loyalty, and sincerity.

Pink Tourmaline's soft color is a bow to feminine strength. The jewel channels feelings of comfort and safety, calming the wearer. The gentle nature of the pink tourmaline can heal emotional wounds and touch the heart.

Prasiolite's leek-green hue strengthens the energy of the soul and mind. It is a reminder to respect and bless one another.

Rose Quartz is the jewel of "gentle love"—from self-love to unconditional romantic love. Compassion, faith, nurturing, and infinite peace describe the stone.

Topaz is named for the Sanskrit word for "fire." This fascinating gem invites respect and affection. Topaz protects against envy and ensures long life.

A Scottish geologist discovered *Tsavorite* in the United Republic of Tanzania and Kenya during the late 1960s. The stone's intense green makes it one of the most popular and expensive garnets.

Tiffany and Co. began designing jewelry set with tsavorite stones in 1974. Tsavorite's color conveys positivity, understanding, wealth, and prosperity. Said to protect travelers, the gemstone promises a life of adventure.

Turquoise is one of the oldest gems set in jewelry. Misnamed the "Turkish stone" by the French, turquoise's actual origin is Persia. Turquoise is celebrated as one of the luckiest gemstones for lovers. Russian jewelers have used gemstones in wedding rings for hundreds of years.

Yellow Diamond's cheerful color creates a sense of joyful optimism, playfulness, and friendship. Bright and sunny, yellow diamonds stand for commitment, devotion, and a pure heart, whether serving to celebrate a new relationship or a continuing one.

Diamonds, sapphires, emeralds, and rubies are the traditional precious stones, but most jewelers categorize all gemstones as "precious" because their supply is limited.

Gemstone cuts' symbolism

A gemstone's shape serves a distinctive purpose. Some believe the cut influences a precious stone's energy. Others contend a jewel's design shows the wearer's personality.

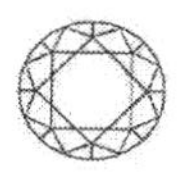

Round cut: This time-honored cut reflects the most light, enhancing a precious stone's sparkle. The round form is classic and indicative of a long-lasting romance and commitment.

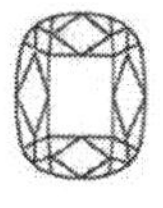

Cushion cut: A vintage cut, the cushion design suggests elegance and romance, with a whisper of old-world luxury.

The "Hope Diamond" is the most celebrated cushion-cut jewel. Its ownership records go back to 1666.

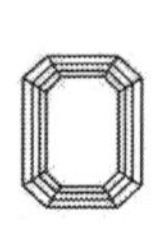

Emerald cut: Jewelers consider the rectangular design of the emerald cut the most formal. One of the oldest cuts, its sleek style was most popular during the art déco period (1920-1930). The elegant look is a nod to modernity, boldness, confidence, and sophistication.

Heart-shaped cut: Nothing says romance like this cut! The heart format is a version of the pear cut and dates to the mid-fifteenth century.

Before the days of jewelry tools, the heart shape was a challenge for gem cutters. Early on, royalty gifted heart-fashioned rings and jewelry as a gesture of goodwill and friendship. The heart contour denotes devotion and love.

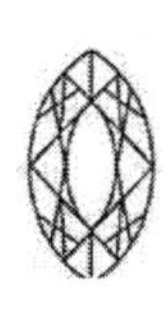

Marquise cut: King Louis XV commissioned the court jeweler to create a shape resembling Madame de Pompadour's (his majesty's mistress) smile. The marquise styling implies joy, glamour, style, and drama—perfect for a person with a daring, outgoing nature.

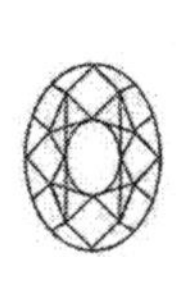

Oval cut: The oval cut, created in the 1960s, appears more significant than a round rock of the same weight. This cut's egg look indicates fertility and children in some cultures, giving it a special appeal. Similarly, the oval represents the birth of a creative and artistic spirit.

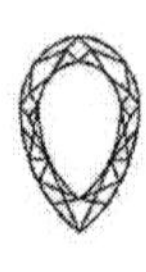

Pear cut: Invented by a Flemish stonecutter in the fifteenth century, the teardrop shape shows adaptability (it looks the same pointing up or down.) The pear cut suggests uniqueness, passion, and adventure.

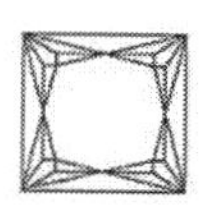

Princess cut: This pattern gained popularity in the 1970s. The edgier style produces an exquisite twinkle. Its lines, symmetry, and sparkle suggest those opting for the princess cut are most likely flirty, trendy, fun loving, and drawn to excitement.

CHAPTER 15

Color Matters

Wedding gown color

An anonymous rhyme of an unknown time asserts that the wedding gown color foretells a bride's fate in wedlock. Superstition? Or life realities of long-ago generations of brides—their truth given voice through the poet's words?

Married in white, you have chosen all right

Married in gray, you will go far away

Married in black, you will wish yourself back

Married in red, you'd better be dead

Married in green, ashamed to be seen

Married in blue, you'll always be true

Married in pearl, you'll continue in a whirl

Married in yellow, ashamed of your fellow

Married in brown, you'll live out of town

Married in pink, your spirits will sink

Even though today's brides may gloss over the lines of harmonizing words, they would be wise to take note of the poet's prophecies when choosing their wedding dress color. For, of all superstitions, those about weddings are the most lasting. Unfounded or not, those beliefs' staying power through hundreds of generations suggests they are deep-anchored in life experience, thus worthy of weighing their worth.

Though the poem's date is uncertain, its content speaks to the social behavior and attitudes of the 1800s' Victorian society:

The rhyme's opening line—*Married in white, you have chosen all right*—could have been influenced by then-reigning Queen Victoria's choice of a white gown (instead of royalty's standard silver) when she married her cousin, Prince Albert in 1840.

Only royalty and the elite could easily afford the expensive bleaching needed to create white, making the color an emblem of wealth.

Gray wedding dresses were socially acceptable and frequently worn during the 1700s. Also, throughout that period, gray was considered suitable for a special occasion or church.

A century later, the color fell into disfavor with the Victorian upper-middle-class and aristocracy because they identified it with their hirelings—housekeepers, personal attendants, scullery maids, etc. Read with that understanding, M*arried in gray, you'll go far away* portrays the 1800s-era privileged classes' attitude that social status determines human value. (But more optimistically, we can assume an alternative interpretation: "Go far away" forecasts that brides outfitted in gray wedding gowns will travel widely!)

Married in black, you'll wish yourself back: The Victorian high-and-mighty banned **black** wedding dresses because the hue is identified with death. Even the wedding guests were forbidden from wearing black.

If the bride or bridegroom's mother wore black at the marriage ceremony, it signaled her disapproval of the couple's union. (And folklore declared that if a bride were garbed in black for her "I do," she would be an unhappy wife, putting the final kibosh on the color for wedding gowns.)

At one time, Roman Catholic brides in Spain wore black to symbolize their "devotion to marriage until death."

Red flashed "scarlet woman" to Victorians. Proper maidens of the day would not have indulged a thought of wearing a red wedding gown. No wonder the frightful warning, *you'd better dead*, appears in the poet's fourth line of verse!

(However, it is traditional for Chinese, Indian, Pakistani, and Vietnamese brides to dress in red for their "big day.")

American brides wore red during the Revolutionary War as a sign of rebellion.

Victorians related **green** to promiscuity. To them, a bride's green dress symbolized "a roll in the grass." That a bride would wear green for her marriage bumped up against English etiquette of the day. The words, *Married in green, ashamed to be seen,* may have been a deep curtsy to the Victorian upper classes' impression that a green wedding dress added up to out-of-wedlock sex.

(If the bride or bridegroom or both is of Scottish-English descent, a green wedding gown is absolutely out! The Scottish-English identify green with Scotland's fabled fairies. Wearing any shade of green could offend the mischievous sprites, who, green with envy, might strike back by stealing the bride away.)

In biblical times, **blue** symbolized heaven, eternity, purity, and faithfulness. (Older, traditional paintings portray the Virgin Mary in blue robes.) By dressing in the color, brides communicated a spiritual connection to the Virgin Mary. That fact alone may explain the line: *Married in blue, you'll always be true.*

As a further explanation for the poet's positive take on blue, the color invites luck, as in the adage, "Touch blue, and your wish will come true."

In 431AD, the Catholic Church color-coded the saints, giving Mary a blue robe, which over time has become known as "navy blue."

The Victorians judged **pearl** and other colors closely resembling flesh as sexually suggestive. They associated the tints with "fast living," thus, *Married in pearl, you'll continue in a whirl* is foretelling endless trouble for the bride's marriage if she wears a pearl color wedding dress.

For many generations before the reign of Queen Victoria, **yellow** was fashionable. But yellow gradually became associated with non-Christians, therefore an unholy color for church wear.

The poem's line, *Married in yellow, ashamed of your fellow*, may show the Victorian churchgoing community's disapproval of wearing yellow for the sacrament of marriage. In general, Victorians were practicing Christians.

Urban Victorians identified **beige** and **brown** with rural locales. The verse *Married in brown, you'll live out of town* seems to say the bride who recites marital vows in brown is unsophisticated and destined to live in the countryside because she lacks the social skills to thrive in an urban neighborhood. Upper classes of the period considered agrarian residents as uneducated and inexperienced.

The final advice, *Marry in pink, your spirits will sink,* is puzzling, especially since **pink** outfits and accessories were popular with Victorian ladies. However, publications of the time encouraged women with fair complexions to avoid wearing pink in the daylight because it would make them appear "sallow" (unhealthy; sickly).

CHAPTER 16

Flower Power

The perpetual pairing

Flowers have been an integral part of wedding ceremonies for over two thousand years.

In the superstitious belief that evil spirits could not penetrate anything resembling a halo, Greek and Roman brides adorned their hair with wreaths of blossoms and aromatic herbs—garlic, dill, and chives.

The protective circlet of ancient times has become today's bridal tiara or bandeau—one more ageless wedding superstition transformed by time into a modern wedding tradition.

Colorful blossoms continue as a prominent feature of formal weddings: ceremony sites are bloom-bedecked, young girls distribute vibrant petals from baskets ahead of brides who carry a bouquet in their hands. And after the marriage vows, a flower arrangement serves as the head table centerpiece at the celebratory reception.

Flowers and the gods

In the 1800s, upper-class Victorian brides chose their wedding flowers based on the blooms' mythical connections to classical Roman gods as much as for their splendor of color. The belief that roses' striking beauty came from their link to Venus and Aphrodite made them a favorite.

Orange blossoms symbolized fertility and abundance (the orange tree bears both a flower and fruit at the same time). Like roses, the orange tree's blossoms boast a connection to a Roman goddess—Juno, the goddess of marriage. Juno gave Jupiter orange blooms on the day they wed.

Superstition says only the bride should wear orange blossoms, and that it's unlucky for anyone else in the wedding party to do so.

Perhaps the most famous couple to ignore the orange blossom curse was former "first lady" Jackie Kennedy and Greek shipping magnate Aristotle Onassis; both wore a crown of orange blossoms at their 1968 marriage.

Floriography: the flower language

People have used blossoms to convey emotions throughout history. As early as the 1600s, people in Persia and the Middle East used flowers to "speak" with each other.

In his 1727 memoir, a Frenchman who lived in Turkey referred to a secret code used by the Turks in which flowers replaced words. The book gave birth to French and English dictionaries defining the meaning of different blooms and leading to what would become known as "floriography," the language of flowers.

The published letters of Mary Wortley Montagu, wife of a British diplomat stationed in Turkey during the 1700s, ignited the Victorians' interest in flower communications. Lady Mary wrote about the hidden way women in harems used flowers to exchange a few words.

England's Victorians enthusiastically read dictionaries and books on floriography. Amorous British gentlemen's curiosity about the "messages" conveyed by various blooms quickly grew into an obsession to "speak" the language.

A poem printed in the latter part of the nineteenth century highlights the classic Victorian romantic's attitude toward floriography:

There is a language, little known,
Lovers claim it as their own
Its symbols smile upon the land,
Wrought by nature's wondrous hand;
And in their silent beauty speak,
Of life and joy, to those who seek
For Love Divine and sunny hours,
In the language of the flowers.

(The Language of Flowers, 1875)

Floriography and romance

Formal etiquette and elegance in romance defined gentlemen of Victorian times. Sensitivity of words and a show of respect for women were the marks of the male aristocracy.

Victorian suitors could express feelings with blossoms they may have been too shy to voice. Floriography formalized flirtations. Flowers could be a non-invasive statement of attraction and less painful rejection.

Suitors gave painstakingly arranged herb and flower bouquets, called "tussie mussies" and "nosegays," so named because they disguised offensive body smells of the time, to their lady of interest. If she held the bouquet to her heart, the suitor's pursuit was welcome, but if she turned the nosegay downward, it signaled absolute disinterest.

Floriography's popularity in Victorian England fascinated the American upper classes. Publishers in the United States churned out flower dictionaries, magazine articles, and books about nonverbal messages. But America's interest in floriography never matched the Victorians' enthusiasm for the flower language.

Floriography has long ago disappeared. Yet flower power is eternal: Blossoms will always be a part of weddings, and a red rose will forever bring a message of affection.

Note: Please see Appendix for *Definitions: Good and Bad Luck Flowers and Herbs*

Flower color hallmarks

Types of flowers, like every classification or category, have specific characteristics. Still, the color of a particular group of blossoms in the *same* family changes that group's original meaning.

For example, red roses symbolize love and passion, but the pink variety conveys friendship. "Messages" associated with each color are:

Flower Color	Symbolism
Blue	Peace, poetry, truth, wisdom

Brown	Calmness, earth, security, support
Gray	Friendship, maturity, responsibility, sorrow
Green	Abundance, healing, hope, money, new beginnings, youth
Gold	Good health, optimism, wealth
Indigo	Spirituality, wisdom
Lavender	Charity, dreams, peace, serenity
Orange	Creativity, happiness, opportunities, power
Pink	Beauty, friendship, harmony, remembrance
Red	Courage, action, faith, life, passion, strength
Silver	Endurance, freedom, reality, restoration
Violet	Forgiveness, humility, intelligence, justice, religion, truth
White	Kindness, purity
Yellow	Creativity, healing, intelligence, intuition, life, light

Birth month flowers

Like birthstones, we associate the months with a blossom or two, each with a special significance. The linkage of each month with flowers likely dates back to the Romans since we consider them the first to celebrate birthdays with blooms.

A birth month floret in bridal arrangements or bouquets adds a personal touch. If one or more suitable blossoms are unavailable, a wedding month flower can be a meaningful option.

Birth Month	Flower/Alternative	Symbolism
January	Carnation/	Admiration, love, health, beauty
	Snowdrop	Friendship, imagination, hope, spiritual confidence
February	Violet/	Modesty, peace, shyness, love, faithfulness, healing
	Primrose	Beauty, youth, grace, healing, pensiveness, protection
March	Daffodil	Esteem, inner power, self-love, gracefulness, good taste
April	Daisy/	Cheerfulness, faithfulness, innocence, intellect, purity, youthful beauty, simplicity
	Sweet pea	Blissful happiness, courage, shyness, strength, tenderness, affection
May	Lily-of-the-valley/	Happiness, humility, mental ability, purity, sweetness
	Hawthorn	Chastity, desire, hope, luck in fishing, protection for ships
June	Rose/	Eternal friendship, love, gladness, healing

Birth Month	Flower/Alternative	Symbolism
June cont.	Honeysuckle	Affection, domestic happiness, fidelity, generosity, psychic powers, sweet disposition
July	Larkspur/	Ardent attachment, brightness, flights of fancy, health, humor
	Water lily	Eloquence, purity of heart
August	Gladiolus/	Courage, generosity, natural grace, strength of character
	Poppy	Dreaminess, eternal sleep, extravagance, imagination, love, luck, money
September	Aster/	Charming, content, dainty, feminine, patient, lucky in love
	Morning glory	Extinguished hope, insincerity, uncertainty, transience
October	Marigold/	Despair, prophetic dreams, uneasiness
	Cosmos	Joy in life, modesty, affection, peacefulness

Birth Month	**Flower/Alternative**	**Symbolism**
November	Chrysanthemum	Abundance, cheerfulness throughout life, love, peacefulness
December	Holly/	Enchantment, foresight, goodwill, dream magic, transformation
	Narcissus	Egotism, childishness

CHAPTER 17

Lucky Omens

"If a black cat crosses your path, it signifies that the animal is going somewhere."

- Groucho Marx

Humankind always wants answers to the inexplicable, therefore, the fascination with superstition. Broadly speaking, superstition explains the unexplainable.

Magic, omens, lucky charms, and rituals—all have been used to explain baffling happenings. Folklore and old wives' tales declare animals, weather, and objects are the reason an event happens or the harbinger of an event to occur in the future.

Looking on the sunny side, we'll start with some good omens.

Animals and insects

- If a cat nearby to the bride sneezes, it's good luck.
- If the bride sees a black feline, lambs, spiders, white birds, elephants, gray horses, or toads on the way to the church or while leaving the marriage ceremony, she can expect to enjoy prosperity and happiness.
- A bride who wakes up to birds singing on her wedding day will be lucky in marriage.

- It is good luck for the bride to allow a cat to eat out of her shoe if she wears the identical shoe at the altar.
- Doves represent love and faithfulness. (White doves choose one partner for life.)
- If the bride or groom sees a gray horse on the way to the marriage ceremony, it means good things will come to the newlyweds. (Gray horses pulled Prince Harry and Meghan Markle's wedding carriage.)
- A butterfly fluttering near a bridal couple ensures a joyous marriage.
- A spider on the bride's dress is good luck. (In the Middle Ages, spiders helped get rid of flies that caused disease.)
- Tell the bees about the wedding; decorating their hives will bring fast fortune to the newlyweds.

On the way to church

- For good luck, the groom should arrive at the church before the bride.
- The bride and groom will have great luck if they ride in a gray car on their way to their marriage. (A black car is the color of a hearse and mourning.)
- If a bride sneezes on her wedding day, it signals a joyful marriage. (Presumably, the more sneezing, the more happiness!)
- For good luck, when leaving home for the marriage ceremony, the bride and groom should exit their front door right foot first and not look back.
- The groom will find luck if he gives a coin to the first person he meets on his wedding day.
- If the bride kisses a baby's head on her "big day," it will guarantee her fertility.
- A chimney sweep's kiss of the bride brings fantastic luck to the marriage. (The kiss sweeps away evil spirits from the fireplace hearth, which represents the heart of the family.)

When Queen Elizabeth married Prince Philip in 1947, an aide to the royal family ushered a chimney sweep into Buckingham Palace to shake the Prince's hand for good luck.

Charms

- ★ Placing a coin in one of the bride's shoes brings prosperity to the wedding couple.
- ★ A sugar cube inside the bride's wedding glove will make the marriage sweeter.
- ★ The groom should carry a miniature horseshoe in his pocket with the prongs turned upward so his good fortune won't run out. (All metal, especially iron, wards off evil.)

- ★ Salt carried in the shoe, pocket, or glove is good luck. It is a reminder that life may be bitter sometimes; nevertheless, the newlywed couple will manage.

The ancient Greeks considered salt a symbol of loyalty and lasting friendship.

The ring

- ★ A clergy member's blessing of the nuptial rings protects the married couple against disease.
- ★ It's a good sign if the wedding band is a perfect fit. If it's too loose, the merger will fall apart, and if it's too tight, the marriage will be stifling.
- ★ Good luck will follow the bride if she kisses her wedding band before it's slipped on her finger.
- ★ A sapphire wedding ring brings endless joy to the marriage.
- ★ An aquamarine gemstone in a wedding ring ensures a long and successful marriage.

Bride's attire

- ★ A bride will have wealth in her marriage if she wears part of her grandmother's wedding veil for her wedding. (An older veil is luckier than a new one, especially if it's a family heirloom.)
- ★ If a happily married woman places the veil on the bride's head, her marriage will be blessed with tremendous fortune.
- ★ An accidental tear in the bride's veil brings happiness.
- ★ If a bride wears a silk wedding dress, she will enjoy good fortune.
- ★ To guarantee good luck, a bride should sew a few of her fiancée's hairs into her wedding dress.
- ★ Pearls will bring great luck to the bride if the gem is her birthstone.
- ★ Sew the last stitch in the wedding dress before the bride walks down the aisle to ensure that the marriage has good luck.
- ★ If the bride wears gold earrings for her wedding, her marriage will be joyful.
- ★ The marriage will be blessed with good luck if the bride places her right arm into the wedding gown's right sleeve first when dressing for the ceremony.
- ★ Ribbons on the bride's bouquet bring good luck. (Blue ribbons ward off evil spirits.)
- ★ Good fortune comes to the person who gets a pin from the bride's gown.

Groom's attire

- ★ It's lucky for the groom to wear his fiancée's birthstone.
- ★ A groom should place something silver in his shoe to ward off fairies; they like to disrupt a wedding.
- ★ The groom should put money, bread, and garlic in his pocket. The first two are for good luck, and the garlic protects him from witchcraft.
- ★ A groom's perfectly centered tie or bowtie means he will be faithful.

★ Gray is the luckiest color for grooms to wear.

Time and weather

★ For great luck, marry in the morning.
★ Sunshine on the way to church is good luck.
★ Wedding day snow means fertility and wealth for the bride and groom.
★ A full moon on a bride's wedding day promises happiness in marriage.
★ Saying the marriage vows when the clock's minute hand advances past the half-hour—for example, at 10:35 in the morning or 4:45 in the afternoon—is good luck. (Upward movement brings blessings because the hand is ascending toward heaven.)
★ If the bride or groom sees a rainbow during their journey to the church or when leaving the wedding ceremony, they will have a joyful marriage.

The ceremony

★ It is lucky for a bride to cry on her wedding day—her tears wash away all sorrows—leaving only happiness.
★ A home marriage ceremony means good luck for a newlywed couple.
★ If the bride and groom stand close together at the altar, witches cannot sneak between them and curse the marriage.
★ Holding hands during the wedding ceremony will bind the couple together forever.
★ Newlyweds will have good fortune if the marriage officiant gets an odd number of dollars for presiding.
★ For good luck, a bride should enter the church with her right foot.
★ The bride should enter and leave the church through the same door to guarantee good fortune in marriage.
★ It's good luck for the bride to carry her mother's prayer book.

- ★ A child crying during the marriage service means good luck.
- ★ For best of luck, the bride and groom should not sing at their wedding!

After the ceremony

- ★ For a happy and healthy future, the bride should exit the church and enter her new home with her right foot.
- ★ To have a long marriage, the bride should break a piece of glassware into as many slivers as possible. (The number of broken pieces represents the number of happy years the married couple will spend together.)
- ★ After their wedding, a bride should be the first to call her husband by name; it guarantees good fortune in their marriage.
- ★ Newlywed couples should release two white doves after the marriage ceremony to make their love and joy last. (Also, freeing a pair of doves wards off evil spirits.)

The honeymoon

- ★ For good fortune, a bride should take something borrowed on her honeymoon.
- ★ It is the best of luck for the newlyweds to keep their honeymoon destination a secret.
- ★ To be sure the bride and groom enjoy a happy honeymoon, tie the bride's suitcase with a white ribbon.
- ★ It is good luck to spend the first night of marriage away from home.

An old Italian proverb says, "A bride who goes to Rome and sees St. Peter's dome will have a happy home."

- ★ An ocean voyage honeymoon is an omen of a long marriage.

★ Newlyweds should sleep facing north on their first nuptial night to guarantee their marital happiness.

Wedding gifts

★ It brings good luck if the first wedding present to arrive is silver.

★ The gift of a wooden spoon means the bride has cooking skills.

★ If the groom gives his bride an engraved silver teaspoon, it will ensure they will never be without food.

★ Candlesticks confirm newlyweds will always have light in their home.

★ A gift of salt and pepper shakers guarantees the newlywed couple will always have food on the table. An alcoholic beverage gift will bless the bride and groom with health and happiness.

★ A bell as a wedding gift symbolizes harmony.

★ It brings good luck for newlyweds to receive money in odd number amounts for wedding gifts.

Chapter 18

Unlucky Omens

A bad omen is a warning. A sign to stop and reconsider. Proceed with caution.

- Kelley Armstrong

Animals

- It's a dreadful omen to see an open grave, a pig, a lizard, owl, or a hare on your wedding day.
- If a bride hears a howling dog or a rooster crow at the break of dawn on the day of her wedding, it's bad luck.
- It's an evil omen if a bat intrudes on the marriage ceremony.

On the way to church

- Seeing a monk or nun on one's wedding day brings bad luck. (A monk or nun indicates a barren life and poverty in the marriage.)
- It means bad luck if the bride passes a funeral procession when she is on her way to the church for the wedding.

The ring

- If the bride buys her wedding ring, she will have an unhappy marriage.

- ★ If the bride or groom loses a wedding band before the marriage, the couple will have poor luck.
- ★ A bride should not allow another woman to try on the engagement ring. The good luck attached to the ring may go away with that person.
- ★ It is bad luck to buy an engagement ring and a wedding ring at the same time.
- ★ If a bride loses her engagement or wedding ring, it means the couple will separate.

Bride's attire

- ★ It's awful luck for the bride to make her wedding dress.
- ★ The marriage is jinxed if the bride's gown was worn or purchased for a prior wedding ceremony.
- ★ A satin or velvet nuptial gown will bring poverty to the marriage.
- ★ The bride's gown should not have a pattern (vines and birds within the fabric pattern foreshadow terrible luck).
- ★ It is unlucky to remake or dye the wedding dress.
- ★ A tear in the bride's wedding gown on the day of the ceremony is an unlucky sign for the marriage.
- ★ For good luck, the bride should not try on her complete wedding outfit before her big day.
- ★ Folklore says if a bride looks in a mirror when dressed for her wedding, part of her soul enters the reflection, and she cannot give all of herself to her groom.
- ★ If the bride loses her garter before the ceremony, her husband will be unfaithful.
- ★ Wearing peep toe shoes or sandals on her matrimonial day means luck is running away from the bride.
- ★ It's unlucky for a bride to show her veil to anyone except her family before the wedding.

- ★ If a bride eats while dressing for the wedding ceremony, the marriage will have bad luck.

Time and weather

- ★ A wedding after sunset foreshadows a troubled married life.
- ★ It is bad luck for the bride to start down the aisle on time.
- ★ Marrying during a leap year means trouble for the wedding couple.
- ★ Cloudy skies and wind on the wedding day may mean a stormy marriage.
- ★ A newlywed couple's fortunes will decline if the ceremony is after a full moon.

The ceremony

- ★ Postponing the wedding date means the marriage will have a troubled future.
- ★ It's bad luck if church bells ring during the ceremony.
- ★ It is unlucky for the groom to see the bride the night before or on the wedding day before she walks down the aisle.
- ★ If the same member of the clergy presides at two weddings on the same day, one couple will have an unhappy marriage.
- ★ It's bad luck for a bride to read the marriage service before the ceremony.
- ★ If the presiding official sneezes during the ceremony, the marriage might be stormy
- ★ Double wedding ceremonies foretell unhappiness for one couple. (If twins marry on the same day, their marriages should take place in separate churches.)
- ★ A bride should think twice before choosing a redhead as a bridesmaid; she could steal the groom.

Wedding gifts

- ★ Newlyweds should never give away a wedding present, for it will bring bad luck.
- ★ Knives, scissors, or anything that cuts are awful wedding gifts, as in the saying: "If you wish strife between a man and his wife, present them with a silver knife." (Sharp objects represent the cutting off of a relationship. To avoid misfortune, give a penny to the gift-giver, changing the gift to a purchase.)
- ★ Brides should not accept a comb as a wedding gift; combs are bad omens because they are popular with witches.
- ★ An alarm clock is on the "never" gift list because "alarm clock" in Chinese sounds like you are sending someone to their ultimate resting place.

- ★ Brides should refuse shoes and suitcases as gifts. Both items suggest the bride or groom will leave the marriage.
- ★ If a bride buys a watch for her groom before the wedding, the marriage will last a short time.
- ★ If the bride accepts perfume as a wedding gift, she desires someone other than her groom.

Other unlucky omens

- ★ If the bride and groom have surnames that begin with the same letter, ill fortune will follow the marriage. ("Change the name and not the letter, marry for worse and not for better.")
- ★ It is tempting fate if the bride writes or signs her married name before her marriage.
- ★ If it's a Scottish wedding, it's bad luck if the bride or groom eats green vegetables that day.
- ★ If the bride accidentally breaks a dish at the wedding reception, it's a sign the marriage may break up.

★ A bride should avoid crossing running water; otherwise, her married life will be rocky.

★ If a dog runs between the newly married couple, it signals bad luck to come.

★ Taking separate wedding photos of the bride and groom means the couple will part.

CHAPTER 19

Lucky or Unlucky Omens: Take Your Pick

Even though they deal with the same subject matter, different wedding superstitions sometimes predict contradicting outcomes—i.e., lucky versus unlucky. Opposite results are typical in superstitions that involve pearls, wedding rings, and weather.

Pearls

Queen Elizabeth II, Princess Diana, former First Lady Jacqueline Bouvier Kennedy, and Monaco princess (and former actress) Grace Kelly wore pearls on their big day. (In Kelly's opinion, "the pearl is the queen of gems and the gem of queens.")

Before diamonds were well known, pearls were *the* "wedding gem." The beads have more symbolism than any other precious stone.

Ancient civilizations believed brides ensured marital happiness by including pearls in their marriage ceremonies. The Greeks thought pearls encouraged marital harmony: the gem symbolized purity, integrity, and fidelity.

★ If the bride dreams of pearls the night before her wedding, she will have a happy married life.

- ★ For each pearl a bride wears, her husband will give her cause for crying.
- ★ If a bride wears pearls on her big day, she will not shed tears in her marriage. (The ancient Greeks regarded pearls as the tears of the gods.)
- ★ It is bad luck for a groom to give his bride pearls on their wedding day.

The wedding ring

- ★ If the bride or groom drops a wedding ring during the marriage ceremony, it shakes off evil spirits hiding in the ring and assures the couple will enjoy a long and love-filled life together.
- ★ A wedding band dropped during the nuptial ceremony signals the marriage will be marked by fighting between the husband and wife.
- ★ If the officiant is the one who retrieves a dropped wedding ring during the wedding service, the marital couple will have a joyous marriage.
- ★ If a married couple loses a wedding or engagement ring, their relationship will end.

Wedding-day rain

Wedding-time rain superstitions are as plentiful as raindrops in a cloudburst.

On the positive side, most cultures consider nuptial day showers an omen of good fortune: Rainfall on a newlywed couple means the marriage will be blessed with wealth.

- ★ Superstition identifies rain with cleansing, renewal, and fertility—the more rain, the more children!
- ★ Wedding-day rain means the bride will be a terrible housekeeper.
- ★ Rain on the bride's big day means a lasting marriage.

Hindu culture tells us, "A wet knot is harder to untie."

- ★ Rain on the marital party on the way to or from the wedding ceremony means the nuptial couple will bicker during the marriage.
- ★ Wedding-day rain washes away any unhappy memories the bride may have; thus, the future is hers to fill with happiness.
- ★ Rainfall on a nuptial day is an omen of unhappiness and frequent weeping for the wife. ("Happy is the bride the sun shines on and woe to the bride that rains on.")

Part III

Appendix

THE WEDDING ANNIVERSARY

"A wedding anniversary is the celebration of love, trust, partnership, tolerance, and tenacity. The order varies for any given year."

- Paul Sweeney

Wedding anniversaries bookmark a couple's life journey together. Gifts and cards renew the happiness of their wedding day. Anniversary gifts begin with less expensive presents and gradually increase in value to symbolize the couple's growing depth of devotion.

Today, every anniversary year has a product associated with it. But before 1937, couples celebrated only the 1st, 5th, 10th, 15th, 20th, 25th, 50th, and 75th anniversaries with a gift.

The 25th and 50th wedding anniversaries are extra special and often include a silver or gold gift, plus a celebration. In the Germanic area of Europe during the Middle Ages, a husband would crown his wife with a silver wreath on their 25th wedding anniversary and with a golden one on their 50th.

TRADITIONAL (AMERICAN) ANNIVERSARY GIFTS

1st Paper

2nd Cotton

3rd Leather

4th Fruit/Flowers

5th Wood

6th Iron

7th Wood/Copper

8th Bronze/Pottery

9th Pottery/Willow

10th Tin/Aluminum

11th Steel

12th Silk/Linen

13th Lace

14th Ivory

15th Crystal

16th Silver Holloware

17th Furniture

18th Porcelain

19th Bronze

20th China

25th Silver

30th Pearls

35th Coral/Jade

40th Rubies/Garnets

45th Sapphires

50th Gold

55th Emerald

60th Diamond

75th Diamond

WEDDING ANNIVERSARY GEMSTONES

I have always felt a gift diamond shines so much better than the one you buy for yourself."

- Mae West

Like traditional wedding gifts, anniversary gemstones also increase in value, reflecting the couple's bond and durability strength.

Year	**Gemstone**
1st	Gold
2nd	Garnet
3rd	Pearl
4th	Blue topaz
5th	Sapphire
6th	Amethyst
7th	Onyx
8th	Tourmaline
9th	Lapis lazuli
10th	Diamond
11th	Turquoise
12th	Jade
13th	Citrine
14th	Opal
15th	Ruby

Year	Gemstone
16th	Peridot
17th	Watch
18th	Cat's eye/chrysoberyl
19th	Aquamarine
20th	Emerald
21st	Iolite
22nd	Spinel
23rd	Imperial topaz
24th	Tanzanite
25th	Silver
30th	Pearl
35th	Emerald, coral, jade
40th	Ruby
45th	Sapphire
50th	Gold
55th	Emerald, Alexandrite
60th	Diamond
65th	Star sapphire
70th	Diamond
80th	Ruby

Notes: The Gemological Institute of America (GIA) is the source of this list. There is no official 5th or 17th wedding anniversary gift.

WEDDING ANNIVERSARY FLOWERS

We also celebrate wedding anniversaries with specific flowers, each representing a marriage milestone.

Year	Flower and Symbolism
1st	Carnation: Beginning love
2nd	Lily-of-the-valley: Purity, devotion
3rd	Sunflower: Lasting happiness
4th	Hydrangea: Gratitude
5th	Daisy: Loyalty, innocence, and faith
6th	Calla lily: Pure love and growth
7th	Freesia: Good spirit, trust
8th	Lilac: Confidence, youthfulness
9th	Bird of paradise: Joy
10th	Daffodil: Happiness, respect
11th	Tulip: Elegance, grace
12th	Peony: Happy marriage and wishes for good health
13th	Chrysanthemum: Abundance, optimism
14th	Orchid: Mature charm, understanding
15th	Rose: Passion, romance
20th	Aster: Patience, wisdom
25th	Iris: Many beautiful memories
30th	Lily: Devotion, purity of heart, pride
40th	Gladiolus: Sincerity, generosity, remembrance
50th	Yellow roses: Inner joy and enduring love

DEFINITIONS: GOOD AND BAD LUCK FLOWERS AND HERBS

Good Luck Flowers/Herbs

Allium ⊛ Luck
Allspice ⊛ Compassion
Aster ⊛ Beginning
Azaleas ⊛ Temperance
Baby's breath ⊛ Innocence and everlasting love
Basil ⊛ Love and hope
Bay leaf ⊛ Strength
Camellia ⊛ Honesty
Chrysanthemum ⊛ Cheerfulness
Crocus ⊛ Youthful happiness
Daffodil ⊛ Respect
Daisy (Gerbera) ⊛ Innocence
Forget-me-nots ⊛ True love and memories
Forget-me-nots ⊛ True love, remembrance
Freesia ⊛ Calmness
Gardenias ⊛ Gracefulness
Garlic ⊛ Courage and wards off evil
Gladiolus ⊛ Grace
Heliotrope ⊛ Devotion
Hibiscus ⊛ Beauty
Holly ⊛ Good will
Honeysuckle ⊛ The ties of love
Hyacinth ⊛ Young love
Ivy ⊛ Fidelity
Lilacs ⊛ Innocence
Lilies ⊛ Return of happiness
Magnolias ⊛ Sweetness
Marigolds ⊛ Sensual passion
Marjoram ⊛ Joy
Mint ⊛ Protection from illness
Myrtle ⊛ Love
Orange blossoms ⊛ Happiness, fertility, and chastity
Orchids ⊛ Beauty, ecstasy
Pansies ⊛ Magical power
Pine ⊛ Compassion
Poppy ⊛ Imagination and pleasure
Purple irises ⊛ Romance
Ranunculus ⊛ Charm
Red & white roses ⊛ Unity
Red chrysanthemums ⊛ "I love you"
Rhododendron ⊛ Fascination
Rosemary ⊛ Remembrance
Roses (red) ⊛ Love, passion
Roses (white) ⊛ Purity
Sage ⊛ Domestic virtue
Sunflowers ⊛ Power and loyalty
Sweet peas ⊛ Lasting pleasure
Thyme ⊛ Strength
Tulips ⊛ Love
Violets ⊛ Faithfulness

Bad Luck Flowers/Herbs

Carnations ⊛ Rejection, disappointment, contempt
Coriander & Dill ⊛ Lust
Hydrangeas ⊛ Heartlessness
Marigolds ⊛ Drunkenness
Peonies ⊛ Shame
Red & white flowers ⊛ Blood and bandages of WWI
White lilies ⊛ Flowers of the dead
Yellow hyacinths ⊛ Jealousy
Yellow roses ⊛ Jealousy

"If I had a flower for every time I thought of you...I could walk through my garden forever."

- Alfred Tennyson

ACKNOWLEDGMENTS

Many people have directly or indirectly contributed to this book. I want to acknowledge a few and thank them for their encouragement and steadfast moral support.

A heartfelt "thank you" to my dear friends Eve Bowen, Barb Mather, Cheri Wilkerson, and my sister Heather Sion—each came along at just the perfect moment, making suggestions and giving me a little nudge when I needed it. Marilyn Oliveira's moral support and advice were invaluable.

Here's a bow to Roberta Zeta, who designed the book cover, and Dane Smith, who created the original interior illustrations. Kudos to Fifi Klein, whose exceptional organizational and formatting skills were invaluable.

Finally, a hug and "thank you!" to my husband for reassuring me I'd finish the manuscript. He is and will forever be golden.

About the Author

Before turning author with *Something Old Something New*, Cherie Sion's work career was research, initially with a major American newspaper and later as founder and chief executive of a firm specializing in studies for multinational corporations.

Currently, Cherie is working on her next book, based on experiences she and her husband have shared in their yearly renewal of wedding vows in different religions and locations throughout the world.

Cherie and her husband live in Playa del Rey, California.

Sneak Preview:

Renew Your I Do

Introduction

Every year, as soon as we turn the calendar to January, my husband and I go into planning mode: where and how will we renew our marital vows this year? We reassert our commitment to each other annually in private and without fanfare. So far, we've reaffirmed our vows over twenty times—typically in a different religion or belief and sometimes halfway around the world.

We've repeated our vows in a public park, in a synagogue, and several temples and cathedrals, including the National Cathedral in Washington, D.C.

A rabbi, priests and ministers, a Native American chief, a ship's captain, and "Elvis" are among those who have pronounced us husband and wife.

Friends have called our vow renewals enchanting, and many have encouraged me to share our experiences. This book is the story of what inspired us to reaffirm our vows and the journey it has taken us.

I've chosen a few of our renewal services to write about, some for their uniqueness and others for the particular challenge they posed. Our journals helped refresh my memory. Several officiants graciously shared memories of the ceremony over which they presided.

Pierre Reverdy (1889–1960), a French poet (and one of Coco Chanel's many lovers), once said, "There is no love—there are only proofs of love."

Our renewal of wedding vows represents small proofs of the love my husband and I share.

Hopefully, our story inspires you and your soul mate to renew your wedding vows.

CHAPTER 2

Counting Our Blessings

Friends

On a freezing Sunday morning in December, Berrien and I checked out of the Cleveland Downtown Hilton, hurriedly put our suitcases in the trunk of a waiting cab, and rushed inside the car, thankful for its warmth. We were on the way to our yearly renewal of wedding vows.

Initially, we planned to visit relatives in Cleveland's Shaker Heights area and reaffirm our marriage vows in a Shaker ceremony. They named the community for Shakers, so I assumed Shaker places of worship would be there.

After phone call misfires and fruitless leads, I realized a Shaker reaffirmation of our vows was not to be. But during my search for Shakers, I came into contact with an angel named "Ann," who saved the day by arranging for us to have a Quaker renewal of marriage vows in Shaker Heights.

A half-hour after leaving the hotel, our taxi turned into the city's Shaker Heights neighborhood and onto Magnolia Drive, our destination. Stately manors, each separated from the curb by long sweeps of lawn, lined the street.

The cab inched along Magnolia Drive, almost coming to a complete stop in front of each of the street's elegant two-story homes.

As we eased by each home, it occurred to me that some of them might have belonged to Cleveland's industrial barons during the city's heyday in the late 1800s.

Our taxi came to a standstill in front of a red brick two-story house with roof dormers and a striking white door framed by two white columns. A low-profile sign on the carpet of trimmed green grass in front read "Cleveland Meeting of the Religious Society of Friends." A cluster of trees marked the driveway running from the street toward the rear of the property.

We had arrived at the location for our renewal of wedding vows. The ceremony was to take place before the Friends' (Quakers) regular Sunday worship. Ann and I had agreed to meet at the back porch of the home.

The driver turned the taxi up the driveway and parked it close to the back porch, but kept the engine and heater running. He turned off the meter and said, "It's Sunday. Not very busy."

Soon, a second car came up the driveway and stopped alongside our taxi. I could see the driver, a woman, wrestling with several plastic bags and a handbag as she swiveled from behind the steering wheel to exit.

Intuitively, I knew it was Ann and took a box of holiday-wrapped Sees chocolates from my purse. We had purchased the candy the day before at the Los Angeles Airport as a "thank you" present for Ann.

Excited to greet her, I walked toward Ann with the gift-wrapped bonbons in hand. She stepped back, an outstretched palm raised, and warned, "Don't get too close to me—I've had the flu—but thanks so much for the chocolates. Wait until we're inside to give them to me, please. Follow me."

After a grateful goodbye to the cabbie, Berrien and I trailed Ann onto the back porch and into the home. The first room we entered was empty except for a line of coat racks on one wall. I guessed it was a mudroom.

Coughing slightly, Ann motioned with one of the plastic bags she carried toward space under the coat racks. "Put your suitcases there. But you better keep on your coats until I turn on the heat."

The late-morning light danced through a bank of kitchen windows into the hallway, showing our way. We followed Ann down the hall into a spacious rose-colored dining room anchored by a massive unlit fireplace on one wall. She put her handbag and plastic bags on the oversized dining table in the room's center and gestured to Berrien and me to take places at the table.

I desperately wanted to explore the old home but controlled the urge by fixing my view on Ann taking holly branches from one of her plastic bags. She began organizing the holly on the fireplace mantle, placing each piece deliberately and occasionally stepping back to inspect her handiwork.

Satisfied with her holly arrangement, Ann returned to the table and opened another plastic bag, from which she removed a bakery box. Carefully, she lifted a white cake topped with blue bow icing from the container. She placed the cake on the tabletop.

"We have lunch in here after our Sunday meeting. The cake is in celebration of your renewal of vows. I know you have to take a plane back to Los Angeles right after saying your vows, but at least have a piece of cake before you go."

Ann's thoughtfulness overwhelmed me. I wanted to hug her but respected her warning not to get too close.

With an "excuse me," Ann left the room and went toward the front entrance. I heard people greeting each other. I had expected a handful of onlookers at our reaffirmation of vows. Had Ann invited the entire congregation?

Soon, Ann returned with several others in tow. She set about introducing them to Berrien and me.

"This is Connie..."

"I want you to meet Lee, our official greeter."

We exchanged a few remarks, and Lee was off to the home's entrance to welcome each new arrival.

Ann resumed her introductions, slowly and one by one.

"Cherie, Berrien, meet Linda. And David, her son."

"It's my pleasure. David is twelve. Say 'hello,' David."

"Hello."

"Cherie, Berrien, please meet Jim." Ann emphasized, "Jim."

Jim's name was familiar to me. Ann had said she would "check with Jim" before agreeing to the vow renewal.

With a broad smile, Jim shook hands with us, saying, "It's a pleasure to welcome you to 'Friends House.' We're looking forward to witnessing your renewal of marriage vows. We should get started. Ann, I'll show Cherie and Berrien where the ceremony will take place."

Jim took the lead across the wide hallway to the opposite side of the home, where he opened tall twin doors, revealing two blocks of chairs facing each other. I guessed there was seating for a hundred or more. An aisle between the blocks of chairs ran from the doorway to two chairs stationed with their backs to another enormous unlit fireplace.

"What an odd seating arrangement," I thought, but recalled reading that members of a Quaker assembly sit so everybody sees and are aware of each other during their meetings to show their equality.

"This is where we have our meetings. I married my wife in this room a few years ago," Jim said. Pointing to the two chairs next to the fireplace, he continued, "You will sit there. Everybody else will sit in the chairs on either side of you."

I'd read that Quakers do not have an ordained clergy but wondered, "What are Berrien and I supposed to do?"

Sensing a need for clarity, Jim explained, "We believe God is within each of us; we don't have to look outside ourselves. So we come together and worship in silence."

He spoke softly, reverently, "When the Spirit touches you, stand and say your vows. Afterward, if God speaks to someone in the assembly, they may speak."

Congregation members (Quakers refer to each other as "friends") trickled into the room, filling the seats. Each prayed in silence, head bowed.

At Jim's suggestion, Berrien and I took our assigned seats and lowered our heads in prayer.

We sat in silence for thirty minutes or more. Finally, Berrien rose to his feet and extended his hand toward me. I stood beside him. Turning to me, he began:

> "Cherie, every year, I'm grateful for this moment, a special time to honor the joy of our love and our commitment to each other by reaffirming our vows. Admittedly, since our wedding

> was in Turkish, neither of us knows what we originally pledged to each other. But those Turkish words became magical when someone shouted in English, 'Kiss the bride!'
>
> "We couldn't understand the language, but our Istanbul wedding became our magic carpet to affirming our marriage vows every year, occasionally in another foreign language. We recognize the sacred commitments the words symbolize, whether spoken by a priest, a rabbi, an imam, a Native American tribal chief, or a Las Vegas 'Elvis.' The meaning of the words is eternal: I love you, Chérie. I treasure you. I'm grateful for the blessings God has given us.
>
> "In God's presence and before this congregation, I take my friend, Chérie, to be my wife, promising through divine help to be her loving and faithful husband, so long as both of us on earth shall live."

My hands were trembling and cold. I whispered to Berrien, "Please hold my hand." He laced his fingers with mine and gave me a squeeze of encouragement. I faced Berrien and began:

> "Those who know us well would not find today's vow renewal surprising. What is surprising is the sheer number of renewals we've racked up. Even more surprising is how fast time goes when you're having fun!
>
> "'Fun' is how I would characterize our lives together, Berrien. I'm thankful for the pleasures you give me daily: waking up with a smile, holding my hand when we walk, and kissing me good night. Thank you for the over-the-top delights, like proposing to me on your knees in a Ferris wheel carriage in Paris, years after our marriage.
>
> "You combine intelligence, patience, and kindness in a delightful package, tied up with a bow of grace and manners.
>
> "Although I'm not sure what I promised in all of our wedding ceremonies, I am sure in my heart and mind that I love and cherish you. I look forward to coauthoring the next chapters of our lives in our book of 'Forever and After' (this was a

reference to the inscription I had engraved in Berrien's wedding band)."

I let out a slight sigh, and Berrien and I reseated ourselves at the fireplace. We sat with our eyes closed and heads bowed.

A quote from Helen Keller, the deaf-blind author, crossed my mind:

Why do we close our eyes when we pray, cry, kiss, dream?

Because the most beautiful things in life are not seen but felt

only by the heart.

Other than the stirring of a chair and an occasional cough, the room remained silent. Long minute-after-long-minute passed.

Aware of the prayers that surrounded me and the spirituality of the moment, I, too, fell into silent prayer.

A clear female voice softly singing "Kumbaya" broke the silence. Unsure whether to look or to keep my head bowed, I kept still, listening.

Another feminine voice joined in harmony with the first.

Then, silence.

Long minutes passed.

I heard someone move a chair. My eyes flickered open. It was Ann who stood just a couple of feet away from me. Her eyes were tearing, and she seemed to struggle to find her voice. I shared a sympathetic glance with Berrien as Ann searched for words.

"This year has been challenging for me, my in-laws' illnesses and personal problems. But with all the issues I've had to deal with, Cherie and Berrien's vow renewal has been positive, a small bright spot, a little corner of happiness."

Again, I wanted to hug Ann, thank her, and offer her a tissue.

More silence. More long minutes.

Linda stood: "I don't know how you can have a sense of closeness to people you've just met, but I feel close to Cherie and Berrien."

More silence.

Connie rose. She spoke slowly, quietly, but with every word clear.

"When you see love, it makes things a little better. Their love makes us all a little better. and it makes the world a bit better."

Silence. More long minutes passed.

Another friend stood: "I'm blessed sharing their message."

I saw Jim offer his hand to the woman next to him.

Earlier, he had told us, "The vow ceremony will be over when I shake hands with another friend."

I started shaking hands enthusiastically with everyone in reach. And, if they looked the least bit open to it, hugging them, thanking them for witnessing our vow reaffirmation, causing smiles and giggles among the friends.

After my third or fourth handshake and hug, I realized handshaking and hugging were not part of the Quaker meeting protocol. Even so, I was pleased my innocence had allowed me to thank some people in our audience.

No one in the audience got up; everybody stayed in their seats.

What had been a solemn gathering quickly turned into a town hall. Our audience peppered me with questions.

Someone asked, "Cherie, how did you choose us for renewing your vows?"

I'd admitted to Ann that I was looking for Shakers, not Quakers. Not eager to share my flawed Shaker Heights reasoning, I began tentatively.

"I have relatives in Shaker Heights. I thought we could visit them and have a Shaker renewal of vows. With the name 'Shaker Heights,' I assumed lots of Shakers are here."

As I finished saying the first sentences, I noticed a few surprised looks and muffled titters among the audience.

Berrien gave me an encouraging glance. I continued:

"I called various religious organizations and left messages, but I couldn't tell from the names if they were Shakers."

Feeling my explanation needed context, I explained, "We had a house fire this year. It burned to the foundation. The reconstruction took months. Suddenly, it was December, and we hadn't renewed our vows. Insurance claims, contractors, subcontractors, and city inspectors had overwhelmed us for months."

My audience was silent, stony silent.

I resumed, hoping for a sympathetic reaction. "When I received a call from Ann, she was trying to reconstruct the messages I'd left about renewing wedding vows."

Nervous, my voice became a whisper. Then, after a pause, I resumed. Now my voice was firm.

"With all the glitches of rebuilding the burned-out home, Ann's willingness to help was heaven sent. I explained to her that Berrien and I reaffirm our vows in a different faith every year."

Not a sound came from the audience.

With a twinge of embarrassment, I shared my entire story.

"I didn't know if Ann was a Shaker, but I thought it impolite to ask her directly. So instead, I said, 'What is the official name of your church?'

"As she replied, I wrote, 'Cleveland Meeting of the Religious Society of Friends.'

"After hanging up, I looked at Berrien and said, 'I don't know who these people are. But they're all friends.'"

At that, my audience broke out in laughter.

In a loud voice, someone said, "A quick search on Google would have revealed we are Quakers."

I didn't dare share my lack of knowledge about Quakers. Besides, I didn't think there were fundamental differences among Quakers, Shakers, and the Amish. I assumed all three go back to the Pilgrims somehow.

My only exposure to Quakers was the rosy-cheeked man with the black hat on the Quaker Oats box.

When the laughter slowed, I explained, "According to Google, couples marrying in the Quaker religion write their vows. That was appealing. We had never written our vows."

Another friend spoke up, "I think there are only a few Shakers left. They're in Maine. They must be in their nineties. The last one gets all the furniture!"

A half-beat of silence, then a loud chorus of uncontrollable laughter broke out.

I couldn't help joining.

"Shakers adopted children or accepted interested adults into their group to keep their religion alive," someone said in a clear voice above the laughter.

Ann interjected, "My father always said the Shaker religion was a losing proposition."

Again, the room erupted in laughter.

A male voice shouted, "Shakers don't marry! They're celibate."

More softly but firmly and clearly, a female voice added, "You should have done the research."

I cringed; my ego singed. As a researcher by profession, I hadn't done my homework.

Everybody had been so lovely to us. I wasn't taking a chance of offending any of these beautiful people. Instead, I was thankful for them and our good fortune. Our travel arrangements had worked out, despite the Christmas holiday bustle. Then the hotel upgraded us even though overbooked for today's Cincinnati Bengals and Browns games.

Thankfully, now Jim took charge and ended the discussion, explaining Berrien and I had to leave for the airport in a few minutes.

We had a piece of cake with Jim, Ann, and a couple of other "friends." Someone said a taxi was out front.

Carefully hugging Ann, I said, "We're in God's presence, so I'm not worried about the flu. You made our vow renewal special!"

Writing our vows was a wonderful experience. The words are "touchable." They are words we can hold and reread forever.

Thank you Ann, my friend.

Made in the USA
Monee, IL
28 January 2022